Broken Inside!

Breaking Free of Panic

Disorder with Agoraphobia

Michelle Zulkowski

ISBN: 978-1-4303-2401-0

Dedication

This book is dedicated to all those who helped me through my ordeal. Wayne I want to thank you for being there for me every step of the way. Even if I don't show it sometimes I do appreciate everything you've done for me and the kids these past few months. (We've been together nineteen years now and I'm amazed that you haven't left me yet.) Thanks for taking me everywhere and always being by my side. I know it hasn't been easy on you. I am not the easiest person to get along with. I am not used to people helping me and taking care of me. To Kristen thank you for understanding. I haven't been the best mom and I am sorry for that. To Kayli thank you for understanding that mommy isn't always able to do everything. Sometimes I need to be taken care of too. Mom I'm glad you are living with us and have been able to help me through this. Thank you for going everywhere with me even when you didn't really feel like it. By sharing your experiences it's made it easier for me to get help. I know I haven't been the best daughter but I try. To my sisters Heather and Tara you have been there no matter what. We all share the pain of living with an anxiety disorder. I am glad that I can come to you no matter what and you are always there for me. Thank you Karen Favors my therapist for helping me realize that I matter. You cared about me and showed me that my disorder was worth treating. You've given me so much valuable information to help me break free of my disorder. I will always remember your humor. Thank you to Dr. Adam

Brownstein and Nurse Lori for listening to me and not judging me. Thank you for caring about me. Thank you to Marietta & Bob Giles for understanding. Thank you to Martha and Soni for being a friend when I needed one. Thank you to Angie for being my friend all these years.

Without the support from all of you I would not be better today.

My story was taken from my journal entries. It was written during the time of my Panic Disorder. I apologize if my writing isn't perfect. I wrote how I felt at the time.

Dear Anxiety,

I have known you as long as I can remember. I always hated you. When you're around I feel like I'm going to die. I could not be trapped or held somewhere. I ran to get away from you. I have to get away to be safe. Over the years I felt you off in the distance. You always let me know you were there; hiding, lurking. At times I could shrug you off and you'd go away. Other times I felt at peace with myself knowing you were not around. Then out of nowhere you show up sneaking up on me. If I expected you there it wouldn't be so bad but when I least expected it there you are. I learned to feel your presence and keep you at bay. I thought if I let you know that you were there I wouldn't be in trouble. I know that I can never relax. To let go and be free means you will attack. Recently I let you take control. I am at a vulnerable place in my life due to other stress factors. You took advantage of that by taking over. I can no longer keep you at a distance. I know you are there. I feel you every minute of every day. You don't talk to me but I hear what you say. You keep me from being healthy. I can't eat certain foods because of you. I can't eat at certain times because of you. I can't take medication to make you go away because you have me convinced that the meds are the enemy. I listen to your negative comments about every single thing. You tell me that I am sick. My body betrays me because of you. I feel every intricate thing that could possibly be wrong with me. I tense up, my heart races. I fear.

I panic.   No one can help me. I am all alone. I want you to go away. If I let you know I'm afraid you will take control. I cannot lose control. I want you to leave me alone. Please God help me. I want control. I want control.

I feel the adrenaline rush. It's coming and I can't stop it. Oh god, No. My heart races out of my chest. Next, the palpitations come. I start shaking. I'm cold and clammy. I'm going numb. It's too hot. I can't breathe. I need air. I am scared. I am alone. I sense the doom. I am going to die. No one can help me.

Broken Inside…

Most people experience moments of anxiety in their daily life. Anxiety disorders may develop from a complex set of risk factors, including genetics, brain chemistry, personality, and life events. When anxiety afflicts you to a point where you can no longer live your life as you once did that's when it becomes disabling. That's what happened to me. An estimated 40 million adult Americans suffer from anxiety disorders each year. Panic attacks affect up to three to six million Americans, and are twice as common in women as in men. About one third of those get help.

The DSM-IV Criteria for Panic Attack are as follows - a discrete period of intense fear or discomfort, in which four (or more) of the following symptoms developed abruptly and reached a peak within 10 minutes: palpitations, pounding heart, or accelerated heart rate, sweating, trembling or shaking, sensations of shortness of breath or smothering, feeling of choking, chest pain or discomfort, nausea or abdominal distress, feeling dizzy, unsteady, lightheaded, or faint, derealization (feelings of unreality) or depersonalization (being detached from oneself), fear of losing control or going crazy, fear of dying, paresthesias (numbness or tingling sensations), chills or hot flushes.

I grew up unaware of my mom experiencing anxiety attacks. She never sought help. It was never talked about. She medicated by drinking alcohol not realizing that this made the anxiety attacks more prevalent. I realize now that there were no resources available to her.

Broken Inside…

It took her nearly ten years to get to a point where she was able to conquer them and live anxiety free.

I felt anxiety over the years. I thought once I felt the anxiety coming on I could control it and once I did I didn't think about it until the next time I felt it.

I can remember times when I was young that I would go to my Aunt Paula's house and I would experience anxiety to the point where I would hyperventilate. At the time I thought I was homesick and that was why I felt the way I did. I would get scared and my Aunt Paula would come in the room and put a humidifier on. She would sit by the bed and talk to me; assuring me that I was ok. She always made me feel better. I never told anyone that I was having these "feelings." I always kept my problems to myself. As the years went on I kept burying my problems.

When I was fourteen and in ninth grade I can remember again feeling anxiety. I would be sitting in typing class and feel my left arm going numb. I was obsessed with the fact that I was having a heart attack and I was going to die. I would be so scared that I would get up out of class and leave. I would meet up with friends and do whatever I could just to forget about how I felt. I thought if I left the situation I would be able to leave the anxiety behind.

I was twenty seven years old when my boyfriend, Wayne and I moved to Delaware City. Our oldest daughter Kristen was five and I just had my second daughter Kayli. I started feeling anxiety again. I felt very lost in the world. I wasn't working. Wayne was working and I felt isolated at home with two kids. Kristen was in kindergarten so I would walk her to and from school. I spent quality time with my baby yet I felt I was missing something in my life. Anxiety consumed me because I didn't work for two years and spent the majority of my time at home. I felt it lurking around me all the time. I would feel it three or four times a day. I started to have an anxiety attack one day and made my boyfriend come home from work to stay with me. I would wake up in the middle of the night and be afraid to go back to sleep because I thought something was going to happen to me. At times I would be able to leave the house. When I was in a store for instance and I would feel the anxiety creeping in I would leave the store and rush home. I would have this feeling of danger lurking around me. I stayed indoors as much as possible because I didn't want anything to happen to me in public. I didn't want people to see me afraid. I finally talked to my family doctor about it and she told me that I needed to get out of the house. I decided to go to work part-time. I found a job not far from my house and I was able to work my schedule around Wayne's so that one of us was at home with the kids at all times. Working was the best thing for me. I was able to work and not have the anxiety consume me. Over the next few years I had little to no anxiety.

We had moved downstate to Magnolia and after working part-time for two years I felt I was ready to work full-time. I found a job at Chimes, a group home for men with developmental delays. Again I was able to work my schedule around Wayne's so that I could get my forty hours. I had to work every weekend for a year straight. I worked double shifts, back to back double shifts, and holidays. I hardly saw my kids and felt I couldn't keep up with the housework. I was very stressed out. Toward the end of that first year I started experiencing anxiety. At home I would worry about how I was going to handle working all the hours I was expected to work. I started having problems with my breathing. I didn't know how to relax. I couldn't figure out how I was going to work when I was having trouble breathing. I called out sick and did not give my four hour notice. I felt horrible about this and that made me stress even more. I worried myself into an anxiety attack. I was crying hysterically and felt nauseous. I started to have chest pains. I had Wayne take me to my family doctor because I thought I was having a heart attack. After having tests done and my doctor's reassurance that I was ok, I finally managed to calm down. After a few months I decided to quit that job.

I started working full-time at a school for children who have varying degrees of developmental delays. The hours and days off were the same as my kids so I was very happy about that. Over the next three years there I rarely felt any anxiety; until the day that changed my life. My anxiety disorder crippled me to the point that I no longer was able to function. In January of this year I was diagnosed with Panic Disorder with Agoraphobia. I only had a vague understanding of what agoraphobia was. To me it was a person who couldn't leave their house. The disorder is much more than that. My panic attacks became more intense and I became afraid of having them in public. I restricted myself to the house for days at a time because I didn't feel safe outside.

The symptoms of agoraphobia are: fear of being alone, fear of losing control in a public place, fear of being in places where escape might be difficult, becoming housebound for prolonged periods, feelings of detachment or estrangement of others, feelings of helplessness, dependence upon others, feeling that the body is unreal, feeling that the environment is unreal, anxiety or panic attack. Agoraphobia affects about a third of all people with panic disorder. Typically situations that invoke anxiety are avoided and in extreme cases, the person may never or rarely leave their home. Typically, people with agoraphobia restrict themselves to a "safety zone" that may include only the home or the immediate neighborhood. Any movement beyond the edges of this "zone" creates mounting anxiety. Sometimes a person with agoraphobia is unable to leave home alone, but can be accompanied by a particular family member or friend. Even when they restrict themselves to "safe" situations, most continue to have panic attacks a few times a month. People with agoraphobia can be seriously disabled by their condition. Some are unable to work, and they may need other family members, who must do the shopping and run all the household errands, as well as accompany the

Broken Inside…

afflicted person on rare excursions outside the "safety zone." People with this disorder may become house-bound for years resulting in loss of social and interpersonal relationships. Thus the person with agoraphobia typically leads a life of extreme dependency and discomfort. This is what became of my life over these few months.

Broken Inside…

When My Life Changed

February 2006

My worst fear came true today. I had a panic attack at work and had to be rushed to the emergency room by ambulance. I think what may have brought it on was stress. This past school year I had some disagreements with the teacher I worked with. The kids I worked with were challenging to say the least even though I loved working as a Paraprofessional in the classroom. The teacher I was working with had been out sick a total of five weeks. During that time I had to work with different substitute teachers. Some of them hadn't worked with the kids in my class so I had to brief them on the kids and their abilities and behaviors. Whenever we had a substitute in the class whether I was out or the teacher was out the student's behaviors were worse.

I wanted to prove to the teacher that I was capable of running the class without her. I tried very hard to do everything I could to make the class run smoothly. I made sure all the data was collected. It seemed that things got easier over those few weeks and I started to feel I was capable of running the class.

After lunch I was helping the substitute get the students ready for bus time when I felt my heart palpitate. Normally when I feel a palpitation I just go on with whatever I'm doing and don't let it bother me but this time I had another one. I started getting scared so I told the substitute that I had to use the restroom. I wanted to be alone so I could calm myself down. I kept feeling the heart palpitations and by now my fear was escalating. I told the substitute that I wasn't feeling well and I had to go the nurse. She said, "Okay."

I went across the hall to another classroom to let my friend Robin know that I wouldn't be able to help her at bus duty because I didn't feel good. I told her I was going to the nurse. I felt guilty about leaving the substitute alone with the kids but I knew I had to leave the classroom. Once there I told the nurse I was having palpitations and I felt I was going to have an anxiety attack.

She had checked my heart rate and blood pressure and both were high. She instructed me to lie down on the bed and put my feet above my head. I lay on my back with my feet raised like she told me to. My heart was racing out of my chest and I thought at that moment I was going to die. I asked the nurses to call Wayne and tell him what was going on and that he would have to pick Kayli up from school because I knew I wasn't capable of getting up, walking out to the parking lot, and driving myself anywhere. I then asked the nurse if she could go get Robin for me.

We had been friends for about three years and I trusted her as a friend. I wanted someone with me who I thought could help me through this. When she came into the nurse's office I told her I was having an anxiety attack. She tried to keep the conversation light hearted and I asked her to stop talking because it wasn't helping. Finally the paramedics arrived and I asked to be taken to the hospital. They put me on the stretcher and the only thing that kept going through my mind was "Oh my God, I hope no one is watching." I felt embarrassed because everyone would know I was being rushed out by ambulance.

I did see the principal standing outside the nurse's office. She later told me that she was there to keep anyone from walking by the nurse's office. Once on the stretcher I felt very embarrassed and humiliated. I don't ever remember having been driven in an ambulance so I was terrified. I kept telling the paramedic I felt like I was going to pass out because my heart was racing out of my chest. He assured me that if anything happened to me he would be able to help me. I kept apologizing for being like this.

Once we got to the hospital I felt the anxiety lessen. My heart was still racing. I waited on the stretcher in the hall way for the doctor to see me. I was still having heart palpitations but my heart rate was slowly returning to normal. A few minutes later Wayne, Kristen, and Kayli arrived at the hospital. I told them I had a panic attack at work. The doctor ordered heart tests and everything came back normal. I was still having the palpitations. The doctor assured me that the palpitations in of themselves are not harmful. After a few hours I was discharged.

Wayne took us home and I had to call my mom and sisters to

assure them that I was ok because they were worried about me. I called my principal and told her I was ok. That whole weekend I continued having the palpitations.

That Sunday night I called my principal and told her I would not be in on Monday. I wasn't ready to face everyone at work. The idea of having all those people know something happened to me and having to tell them what was wrong was not something I was ready to do. When I went back to work Tuesday those who asked if I was ok didn't pry. I told them I was fine and left it at that.

I didn't have anymore anxiety the rest of the school year. I had off all summer and didn't return to work until August.

I didn't even have any concern about going back to work. I was happy that I would be working with Amy this year. Four of the five children in our class I had worked with before.

During the months of September through December I went through a lot of personal problems. I was feeling overwhelmed with our finances. I started to get behind in the bills. Wayne's work was slowing down and we didn't have as much money coming in. I started to manipulate the money and got further behind in our bills. I borrowed money without telling him and when the money came due we didn't have it.

I would pray every night for God to help us through this financial mess. In my mind more money would've helped us get our bills caught up so we could survive financially.

Broken Inside…

It's funny because over the summer we thought about putting our house up for sale and buying a bigger house. At that time Wayne was bringing in enough money to where we paid our bills on time and was able to save some. We quickly decided not to go through with selling the house because his pay was drastically reduced. I was glad that we didn't buy a bigger house because we would've ended up losing it. We got behind on our mortgage payments and truck payments. We thought we might lose the house. I did contact the mortgage company to work out payment arrangements with them. Thankfully they were willing to work with us. Then we had to figure out how we were going to catch up on the truck payments. All our other bills were piling up and we could only afford to pay certain bills.

I dreaded the thought of Christmas. This would be the first time we ever had to worry about Christmas. I knew we wouldn't have any money for Christmas. The kids were outgrowing their clothes and they needed new clothes. I didn't have the money for those. I felt like a bad parent because I could not provide for my children.

When Wayne got laid off from his job the first time, he found another job in two weeks. I was hopeful that things could get better. They didn't. After a few months he was laid off again. I knew we wouldn't be able to get caught up financially. I tried to act as if everything was fine whenever I'd talk to people. I certainly didn't want anyone to know my whole life was falling apart. It only attributed to the thought that I was having that everything I ever did wrong is what put me in this place I was in.

I was living in hell. I still got up and went to work everyday like nothing was wrong. I lived through other people's happiness by pretending I was someone else. I hated my life and myself and felt everyone else had it better than me. I started to resent everyone else's happiness but even more I resented Wayne because for the first time in my life I wanted someone else to fix things. I felt I had gotten us into this mess and I couldn't figure out a way to fix it. I wanted him to make everything better and he couldn't.

I really started to vent my feelings of anger towards him and contemplated leaving him because I wanted to be by myself. That way I wouldn't be responsible for messing up anyone's lives. I felt especially guilty about not being able to provide for my children. The one thing I always made sure was that my children never went without and that they never felt like I did when I was growing up; less than everyone else.

My mind raced at the thought of; if we lose the car, how are we going to get to work? Our credit is bad now and we can't just go get another vehicle. If we lost the house, where would we live? Would my children end up homeless and in Foster Care? We weren't able to move in with anyone else and we wouldn't want to burden our families.

Broken Inside…

We were on a one-way descent downhill and I couldn't stop it. I refused to acknowledge how this all made me feel. Twice I had thoughts about running my truck off the road because I didn't want to live. I was so completely depressed. I pushed aside all those thoughts and was adamant about only seeing the good in my life. That was the only way I could survive this ordeal. My charade paid off. No one knew the hell I was going through. It got easier and easier for me to get up and go to work everyday if I only acknowledged the good things in my life. Eventually though I would pay a toll.

December 2, 2006

Today we went to the Showplace Arena in Upper Marlboro, MD for Kristen and Kayli's first cheerleading competition this season. I love watching all the teams perform.

Growing up I was never a part of any sport so I am proud that my daughter's are involved in cheerleading. They are talented and confident; I lack confidence and talent. I am proud that my nine year old daughter Kayli is on a level 4 squad. She works very hard and loves what she does. I am proud that she has been able to do this since last year. I am proud that Kristen is in her third year of competitive cheerleading.

At least they have an interest that keeps them focused. Maybe if I would've had that growing up I wouldn't have ended up where I am today. Anyway, it's exciting to watch the teams compete. Today

Broken Inside…

I let go of all my worries and only concentrated on the cheerleading.

December 10, 2006

This weekend we went to Atlantic City, NJ for the East Coast Challenge Nationals Cheerleading Competition. Even though we can't afford it we paid only $79 for our hotel. We packed our own drinks and snacks. We only had enough money to pay our admission and to go out to eat once. To me this was more important than worrying about my bills. Is that bad? Well, we had a great time.

About two weeks before Christmas I had another panic attack at work. That morning while I was in the gym with the kids I could feel the anxiety hovering around me. I tried not think of it and shook it off.

Later when it was time to go to the Occupational Therapy Room I thought I was fine. For about fifteen minutes I was by myself with the kids and I kept feeling the anxiety. I was alone so the anxiety kept coming. I wasn't able to get my mind off of it.

Once Michelle came back from lunch to help me get the kids back to the classroom I thought I would be fine. I wasn't. I was trying to help the kids put their shoes on and instantly the panic intensified. I felt the adrenaline rush. My heart started racing and I felt I had to get out of the room. I told Michelle I was having an anxiety attack and walked out of the room.

Broken Inside…

I walked into another room by myself and started to cry. Susan, the OT Teacher, came in and put her arm around me. She talked to me and told me I would be ok. I started to calm down and for a brief moment thought I might be able to go back to the classroom as if nothing happened. I was wrong.

I knew that I had to leave the building. I could not be around anybody the way I was feeling. I told her to have Mack help Michelle with the kids because I was going home. I felt guilty about leaving Michelle with the kids but I wasn't able to help her. I walked down the hall crying. I went to my classroom and grabbed my purse. I walked to the principal's office and told her I had to leave. I told her I was having a panic attack. She asked me if I was going to be ok. I told her "Yes, but I need to leave and be by myself." I walked out the front of the building and my heart was racing.

I proceeded to my truck and drove myself home. I knew if I stayed in school and asked for help it would make the panic attack worse. I contemplated stopping and picking up Kayli from school but decided against it because I didn't want anyone at her school to know something was wrong with me. I didn't want to go to the hospital.

As I was driving the entire way home I had all of the windows down and the air conditioner on because I kept feeling like I was going to pass out. I kept praying that I would not pass out while I was driving. I just wanted to get home and relax. The closer I got to home the calmer I felt.

Broken Inside…

Once I got there I saw my puppy and started to pet him. I then took a bath and read a magazine to get my mind off the anxiety. After that I went into the living room and watched TV. It wasn't long before my heart rate returned to normal and I was calm. I felt completely exhausted so I took a nap.

I got up and went to pick Kayli up from school. I decided to take off the next three days and not return to work until the following Monday. I called my boss and talked to her honestly about what was going on. I assured her that it wasn't work, or the kids that were stressing me out causing my anxiety attack. I told her I was going through some personal problems and needed to take a few days off to get myself together.

That Monday was very hard for me at work. All day I kept feeling the anxiety all around me. I started to feel shaky and scared.

That afternoon when I was alone with the kids in the classroom I started to feel an anxiety attack come on again. Somehow I overcame it and didn't have a panic attack.

All afternoon as Amy and I were trying to get the kids down for their nap I kept asking Amy if I was going to be ok. She kept replying "Yes." I think she thought I was talking about my life in general. What I really meant was that I was afraid of the anxiety and I was afraid I would lose control and it would take over again.

I appreciated that she cared enough to tell me I'd be ok. That's when I decided to go to therapy.

Broken Inside…

January 3, 2007

I woke up today and knew I wouldn't be able to go into work. I had a nice Christmas break and had no anxiety. The thought of going back to work scared me. I wasn't ready to deal with the kids. I called out sick. I told my boss that I had been sick over break which was true. I felt guilty about calling out but I didn't care.

That night I called the teacher that I work with to see how the school day went. I told her I would be there the next day which was Thursday. Once I got off the phone it bothered me that the kids and their behaviors were stressing me out.

January 4, 2007

When I woke up this morning I had intended on going into work. The more and more I thought about the kids at work the more I thought about the anxiety. I knew I wasn't going to be able to go to work and deal with the kids.

At 8 am I called my boss to tell her that I was taking a leave of absence for personal reasons. She asked me if I was coming in to work today and I told her, "No." She said, "Okay."

When I got off the phone with her I felt so bad that I just did that. I didn't care because I felt this is what I needed to do for me.

Wayne and I took Kayli to school and then I drove over to the district office to fill out the necessary paperwork. I had to also write a letter to go along with the forms. What I had written was the truth. I had the panic attack at work Feb. 2006. I did have the second panic attack at work not long before Christmas. I was dealing with a lot of personal family issues. I did feel broken inside and needed time off to fix myself. The director understood. I hadn't thought about how much time I would need to take off. I put thirty days on the form. I was also given instructions to call about short term disability. When I left the office I felt confident that I did the right thing.

January 5, 2007

After picking Kayli up from school I was going to run into Walmart to pick up a few things. On the way to pick Kayli up I was thinking "What if I run into someone from work at Walmart"? I was worried that they would wonder why I can be in Walmart but not be able to go to work.

I asked Wayne if we could go to Food Lion in Harrington after we picked Kayli up that way I wouldn't run into anyone from work. He didn't want to go there.

We picked Kayli up and I asked him to drop us off at the front of the store. Kayli and I walked into Walmart. I got about halfway into the store when I felt the panic attack come on. I felt the adrenaline rush and my heart starting to race. I turned around and calmly told Kayli that we needed to leave.

As we were walking out she asked me what was wrong. I

said, "Nothing, I'll tell you later." Wayne was still driving around the parking lot looking for a parking spot. He saw us standing out front and pulled up to pick us up. I told him I was having anxiety.

The plan was to go home, drop Wayne off, pick my older daughter Kristen up, and go to the corner store by my house. I was determined that I needed to get these groceries. I was still shaky from the anxiety but felt I was able to drive not far from my house. I told Kristen that I was going to have her and Kayli run into the store for me.

I drove to the corner store. Kristen and Kayli went inside. I could feel my heart racing again. I could see the kids inside the store. I beeped and beeped and told them we had to go. I drove home in a panic.

Once inside I quickly undressed and put on my pajamas. I knew I wouldn't be able to do anything else the rest of the night. I sat on the couch next to Wayne and the panic attack hit me. My heart was racing out of my chest, I started to have the heart palpitations, and I thought I was going to die.

I grabbed the phone and went to lie on the other couch. I put my feet up and called my therapist's office. The secretary told me that she was in with a client. I asked her to have Karen call me because I was having an anxiety attack.

About fifteen minutes later she called me back. I needed her to tell me that I wasn't going to die. She assured me that I would be

Broken Inside…

ok. She asked what had brought the panic attack on and I explained about me taking leave and feeling guilty about it. I told her I was worried that I would run into people from work when I was in Walmart because I always worry about what people think of me. After talking to me for awhile I told her that if I got through this attack I would ask my doctor about putting me on medication. I promised myself I would do that.

January 6, 2007

I wasn't able to do much today. Complete exhaustion takes over anytime I get off the couch. I start to panic anytime my heartbeats increase. I'm afraid to sweep the kitchen floor. I tried to cook dinner. I got about halfway through and I had to have my mom finish it. I started to feel the anxiety building. I sat on the couch and for one brief moment wanted to call 911 because I thought I was going to die. The rest of the day was spent on the couch. I can't do anything. What kind of mother am I?

January 7, 2007

I spent the entire day on the couch resting. I'm afraid to do anything else because I don't want the anxiety to get me.

January 8, 2007

It's Monday morning. The thought of having to get up to get my daughter ready for school terrifies me. I have to force myself to function.

I get up put my contacts in, brush my teeth, and wash my face. I start to wake up a little and I am feeling better about being up and around. I get my cup of decaf tea and relax on the couch until it's time to wake Kayli up. I go upstairs and my heart is racing. I tell myself I'm going to be okay.

Once she's dressed for school I realize that I'm not going to be able to go with Wayne to take her to school. Thank God he's been home with me because I wouldn't be able to take care of the kids by myself. I can't leave the house.

I kiss Kayli goodbye and tell Wayne that I cannot go with him. He understands and they leave. I sit on the couch and cry. I have never been this scared in my life. I am totally depressed and spend the rest of the day on the couch. Why won't the anxiety leave?

January 9, 2007

It's been four days since I've left the house. I feel so useless. Am I losing my mind? I got up this morning and got Kayli ready for school. Wayne had to take her to school because I wasn't able to leave the house. I was afraid of going with Wayne to take her to school. I was afraid that I would have a panic attack on the way to her school. I didn't want to be out in public and have another panic attack so I stayed indoors those couple days.

Broken Inside...

That afternoon I wanted so desperately to be able to go with Wayne to pick Kayli up from school. I sat on the couch and cried while my older daughter Kristen comforted me. She told me that I would be okay if I got in the truck and went with Wayne to Kayli's school.

I had to force myself to walk out the front door. I was shaking. I made it to the truck in the driveway and told myself I'd be fine. I told Wayne to drive the back roads because the idea of sitting in traffic near people terrified me.

I was fine until we came to the first red light. I started to feel the anxiety and took a deep breath. I told Wayne I was having anxiety and he told me I would be fine.

When we got to her school I wasn't able to go in to get her. I couldn't even do that.

January 10, 2007

Today I have my doctor appointment. Today was the first day I've worn regular clothes since Friday (Jan 4th). When I went out yesterday for the first time it was in my pajamas. I've been afraid to take a shower so I washed up in the tub quickly.

After I got dressed I had to sit on the couch to relax. I was starting to feel anxiety. When it was time to leave for my doctor's appointment my heart was racing from fear. Wayne had to drive.

When we got there he had to go into the doctor's office with me. The nurse, Lori checked my blood pressure and it was a little high. That made me more nervous because I've always had a normal blood pressure. I asked the nurse if I passed out in her office would her and my doctor be able to revive me. She said that they would. I explained to her about my anxiety.

She went on to tell me that she also suffers from anxiety and talked about her panic attacks which led her to the hospital. She has since been on medication and is doing much better. It was such a relief to know that someone besides me and my family suffered as well and that there was hope for a normal life.

When the doctor came in I talked to him about my anxiety. I explained to him that I hadn't been able to leave the house, I wasn't able to drive and didn't know when I would be ok to go back to work.

I told him about my taking FMLA (personal leave) from work and he agreed that I not go back to work until February 8, 2007.

He wrote me a prescription for Prozac and Xanax. I had to tell him of my fears of taking the medication. He assured me that the meds would help me and not hurt me. The idea of having to take medication and me not being able to control what it does to me on the inside frightened me. I feared losing control. The anxiety took control and it always made me feel that medication was the enemy. I agreed that I would take the medication. I assured him that I would continue on with my therapy.

Wayne and I left my doctor appointment and went to pick

Broken Inside…

Kayli up from school.

Next we went to Walmart to get my prescription filled. When we pulled into the Walmart parking lot I could feel myself tense up. I didn't know if I'd be able to go in. Wayne assured me that I'd be fine.

I walked slowly into the store. I dropped off my prescription and told Wayne I would wait out in the truck until it was ready.

When it was time to go in and get my medicine I wasn't able to go in. I begged Wayne to go pick up my meds. He came out to the truck and told me I had to pick them up since one was a controlled substance.

I nervously walked back into Walmart. This time I had to wait in a line. Thankfully I didn't wait too long. I got my meds and we went home. I was afraid to start my medication that night so I didn't.

I contacted the Hartford regarding my short term disability. I told them about my anxiety, the panic attacks, and me not being able to leave the house. I didn't want them to think I didn't want to work. I wanted them to know that every aspect of my life was altered now due to my anxiety. I couldn't even drive in the truck anymore. I explained that although I may look normal on the outside I was broken inside. If someone looked at me they wouldn't know there was something wrong with me. I didn't exhibit any visible limitations as most disabilities probably do.

I was told that my illness was just as debilitating as another person's disability. Anxiety is a real illness. They informed me that "you would be surprised how many people go out on disability for anxiety disorders." I wasn't aware that anxiety disorder was considered a disability. I guess when it affects your ability to live a normal life that's when it becomes a disability.

I felt better when I got off the phone. I felt like what I was going through was validated.

January 11, 2007

This morning I was a basket case. I knew I needed the meds to help me get better but I was petrified of having to put a pill in my mouth and swallow it.

I decided to call the nurse at my doctor's office. I felt safer if I could talk to her while I was taking the med for the first time. I left a message on their voice mail for her to call me back.

A few minutes later she called me back. She could tell by my voice that I was experiencing anxiety at the thought of having to take the Prozac. She instructed me to take half of the Xanax because that would calm me down enough to be able to take the Prozac. I did as she instructed. I took half a Xanax and cried to her on the phone. That was the hardest thing for me to do. She told me in an hour to take the other half of Xanax and then take the Prozac.

I got off the phone and sat next to Wayne on the couch. I hoped and prayed I would not have an allergic reaction. I didn't.

Broken Inside...

About forty minutes later I started to feel the effects of the Xanax. A calm that I have never felt before came over me and I was elated. I took the other half soon after and within no time I felt relaxed.

That afternoon I took my Prozac and was so proud of myself. Before picking Kayli up from school Wayne and I went to Dollar General. I felt that I was able to go in there because it was a smaller store and not crowded. I was able to walk around the store without feeling the anxiety closing in on me. I knew in the back of my mind that my anxiety was there but it was suppressed. When we left the store I finally felt like I accomplished something.

January 12, 2007

Today I was a little nervous about taking the Prozac. I ate my breakfast then I took it. For about two hours I was tired and depressed so I took a nap.

Later on Wayne was getting ready to go to the store. As he got near the front door I panicked. He looked at me and asked what was wrong. I told him that I was afraid to be by myself. I wouldn't let him leave and he was mad. I felt guilty about making him stay home with me. I was afraid that I might have some side effects from the medications and didn't want to be by myself if something happened to me.

That night I told Wayne there was no way in the world that I would be able to go to Kristen and Kayli's competition on Saturday.

Broken Inside…

It was in Philadelphia, PA. I wouldn't be able to handle the car ride let alone sitting at the competition for a few hours around all those people. He understood and said he would go without me. His dad was going with them so he wouldn't be by himself.

January 13, 2007

I had to take a Xanax this morning. The idea of having to talk to Wayne's parents when they got to my house scared me. Marietta was dropping Bob off at my house so he could go to the competition with Wayne. She was going to pick Bob up when they got back from Philadelphia.

I got up and helped Kayli get ready for the competition. I made breakfast and told them GOOD LUCK when they left!

I felt like a horrible parent because I wasn't capable of going with them. I had never missed going to any of their competitions.

They left and I was mentally exhausted. I lay on the couch the entire day. I tried not to think about the anxiety. I kept watching television to keep my mind off of it. I was happy that Marietta was coming that evening. It would give me someone to talk to. I was glad I stayed home today.

January 15, 2007

I went with Wayne to the gas station. As I sat in the truck waiting for him to pump the gas I watched an elderly woman of about sixty years old get out of her car. She began to pump her own gas and when she was finished she got into her car and drove off. She did all this by HERSELF. What is wrong with me?

January 18, 2007

Kayli has practice tonight and it's my turn to carpool. I want desperately to go. I told Wayne that I would ride up to Middletown with him but if I had any anxiety could he bring me home? He said, "No." He kept telling me I would be fine riding with him.

As I am getting dressed I am shaking and my heart is racing. I dress slowly and cautiously. I grab my drink, snack, and magazines. I mentally prepare myself for the forty five minute drive. I have driven to their practice many times before but not since anxiety took over.

In the truck I work on my bank account to keep my mind busy. Once we get there I told Wayne that I could not go in. He looks at me like I'm crazy. I have been in the gym many times and am friends with a lot of the parents of the other kids but I cannot get out of the truck.

I sit in the truck for an hour reading my magazines. Finally Wayne tells me that inside the gym doors are the benches and I have nothing to fear.

I warily follow him into the gym. I feel the anxiety heightened and I tell myself I will be fine. I sit near the door and focus on the kids who are practicing. I am so proud because I was actually able to sit there for an hour. I was even able to talk to some of the parents. I never left the vicinity of the door and never told anyone there what I was going through.

January 20, 2007

Today my sisters Heather and Tara are coming to spend the night. I want a chance for my mom, sisters, and me to talk about what was going on in our lives. My sister Heather had been suffering from anxiety, was taking medication, and just started therapy. Tara had been suffering from anxiety and also has had panic attacks. My mom had suffered with anxiety for over ten years. I want to be able to talk to them and talk about how therapy was/wasn't helping me.

I kept telling myself that if I had anxiety when they came I would take a Xanax and leave the room. As long as I had an escape I think I will be ok. I kept telling myself that it was no different than any other time they've come over.

Wayne agreed to take Kayli out for the day and for them to remain upstairs when they get back so we could talk. Kristen went to her friend's house.

Things went well. My mom answered a lot of questions about my childhood. Although I have a clearer view of myself as a baby and learned a lot about my father I still don't have the underlying question answered.

Broken Inside...

I started to feel this week that my anxiety has taken on a life of its own. When I was talking to Wayne about it the other day he made the comment, "You talk about your anxiety like it's a person." He couldn't have been more correct. I do feel that anxiety is a separate entity. I feel that it's waiting to attack me when I least expect it; in some way that makes me feel more in control because if anxiety is an actual person I can face that person more easily than I can face the anxiety if it is a fear deep inside me. I think maybe the fog will be lifted. I can only hope.

January 21, 2007

I made it through the night without any anxiety. I am so proud of myself. It was nice to get together with my mom and sisters.

January 22, 2007

Kristen had practice tonight. I went with Wayne to drive her there. After about a half an hour driving I felt this catastrophic feeling that I wouldn't be able to sit at the gym for two hours while they practiced and then sit in the truck for forty five minutes for the drive home. I felt the walls closing in on me. I kept sensing the doom coming. I told Wayne that I would have to go home once we took Kristen to practice. He told me that I would be fine at the gym. I tried not to listen to the thoughts in my head. I did end up sitting at the gym and rode home with no problem.

Broken Inside…

January 25, 2007

    I had therapy this afternoon. Wayne and I picked Kayli up on the way there since she had a half day. After they dropped me off Wayne and Kayli were going out to lunch. I had a little anxiety during my session. I had told Karen about my book, "Nobody Special" that I had written and am in the process of having edited. It's about my life experiences and how I went from child victim to adult survivor. My dream in life would be to have it published and make a difference in the world.

    Karen wants me to write on a piece of paper "New York Times Best Seller" and put the title of my book on the number one spot. I think this is silly because I know that my book will never make it on the New York Times Best Seller List let alone be a number one best seller.

    I humor her and tell her to give me a piece of paper and I'll do it for her. She tells me, "No." I have to do it at home. "Whatever, I think to myself." I ask myself how this is supposed to help me get rid of the anxiety and get better. She tells me that by envisioning this I have the power to make it happen. I am told positive thoughts produce positive reactions. I'm not convinced that this will help me get better and be able to get my life back together. I tell her I'm getting by just functioning. She asks me if I want to merely function or live my life. Good question. Of course I want to live my life but right now I'm not able to do that. I don't trust her. Can she help me?

Broken Inside…

That night I do as she asks. I went to the New York Times Best Seller website and printed out the top five books on the list. I then typed my book title and synopsis to look exactly like theirs. I pasted my copy onto the paper and it looks just like my book is number one. Wouldn't it be nice if that actually came true?

January 26, 2007

Today I went with Wayne to pick up Kayli from school. I still can't drive by myself but I was able to walk into Kayli's school today to get her. I felt the anxiety when I walked into the cafeteria. Since I knew I'd be right out I knew I'd be ok. She asked me if all those people being in the cafeteria made me nervous and I replied, "Yes."

Afterwards we went to the library so I could drop some books off that were due back a few weeks ago. I was nervous about having to walk into the library by myself but I knew I had to do it. Lucky for me there was a drop slot outside the building.

Wayne and I then took Kayli to Smyrna for a friend's birthday party. Since we were a little early and I hadn't gotten her a gift we went into Rose's Department Store. It's not as big as Walmart so I thought I could walk around the store. I told myself that if I felt the anxiety I would calmly walk out to the truck. I knew that I had my medicine on me so I felt a little at ease. I was able to walk around the store.

We decided to get something to eat since we had a little time until the party started. We were going to go to Pat's Pizzeria but there was a line waiting to get in. I told Wayne that I couldn't go in there.

We decided to go into this little diner next door. Once we got inside and I saw all the people sitting around me I felt shaky. I told Wayne that I would not be able to eat in front of all those people.

I ordered my dinner to go and told Wayne that if I needed to leave I would go sit in the truck. It took a lot for me to be able to sit there and wait for the waitress to take our order and for them to finish eating.

Finally they were done and I was happy to leave. We had only been in there about twenty five minutes. It felt like hours.

Afterwards it was time to go to the party. We arrived there and I ran into a friend from work. I didn't tell her what exactly was wrong with me just that I was doing better and it was a personal medical thing I was going through.

We dropped Kayli off at the party and her friend's mom was going to bring her home. Once we got in the truck I was again mentally exhausted. I went home and ate and then went to sleep.

January 27, 2007

I decided that I was going to go with Wayne to the competition. We were going to the Lia Couras Center at Temple University in Philadelphia, PA. I had to take a Xanax and once it kicked in I was relaxed.

Broken Inside…

We got to the competition about noon. Their awards ceremony was at 4:20. I was able to walk down the rows of seats in the arena. Wayne and I sat close to the competition floor. When it was time for Kristen and Kayli to compete I walked down to the floor and was able to sit next to the other parents. I videotaped their performances and then went back and sat next to Wayne.

About 4:00 I started to feel the room close in on me. I told Wayne very calmly that I needed the keys because I was going out to the truck. Kristen and Wayne gave me this strange look and I said, "I need to go now." Wayne gave me the keys and I proceeded to walk up the stairs and out of the arena by myself. The thought of walking out of the arena with all those people once the awards ceremony was over gave me anxiety.

I walked calmly to the parking garage and up the elevator to my truck. I knew if I would've panicked I would've had a panic attack. I told myself I was fine and proceeded to my vehicle.

Once inside I felt safe. I read a magazine and munched on some pretzels. About an hour later Wayne and the girls came out of the arena. I told them I was fine I just needed to get out of there. I had had enough of it.

January 28, 2007

Today my daughters had a competition at the Showplace Arena in Upper Marlboro. I had been there before so in my mind as long as I sat in the area closest to the main door I would be okay. I also gauged in my mind the distance from the building to where our truck was parked. I knew that I could make it to the truck if panic took over. The walk from the arena yesterday to the truck was a lot further away than where we were parked today. Plus this competition was only three hours long including the awards ceremony whereas yesterdays' competition was longer. I knew I had lasted four hours yesterday so I felt confident that I would last three hours and be able to sit through the awards ceremony.

Of course I had to take a Xanax before we arrived. Once there I was calm. Because the competition floor was a lot further away from where our seats were I chose to stay in my seat to watch the competition. Usually when we go to a competition I like to walk around the vendors and browse or get something to eat but I am not able to do that now.

I made it through the awards ceremony and was even able to walk out of the arena with everyone else. I accomplished a goal today.

January 29, 2007

Today I am completely, mentally drained. I couldn't go with Wayne to drop Kayli off or pick her up from school. I even told Wayne that I couldn't go with him to take Kristen to practice tonight. I literally lay on the couch all day and napped throughout. If I'm this exhausted from just these past three days where I really haven't done much other than sit in the truck and sit at the competitions for no more than four hours how am I going to be able to go back to work February 8th?

February 5, 2007

I've had a lot of guilt about being out of work.

Last night I dreamt that *I was outside on a beautiful, sunny day. I was outside of my work behind the school. I was talking to a few people from my work. The next thing I am sitting on a swing. I am swinging on the swing and I can feel my hair blowing in the wind. I am completely at peace feeling the sun on my face. My eyes grow heavy and I feel myself relaxing. I start to drift off to sleep. As I start to wake up I realize that I am still on the swing but I'm in a dark tunnel now. I see a lot of people scurrying around. They begin to walk up these steps into this house. I follow them. At first we are walking through all these different rooms and then I step into this particular bedroom and it looks like it's been deserted. I look around the room and see the two beds on opposite sides of the room and I look at the pictures on the walls. I open the door of the room and see straight ahead a vending machine. As I look to my left and right I realize I'm in a hospital. I continue on my journey and begin to talk to one of the patients. I don't realize until after I am talking to him that I am in a mental institution. As I make my way through the*

corridors I see a fat man lying naked on a hospital operating table.
Attached to him is a small girl who is also naked. She is stuck to him
in a sexual position. I am baffled by this. She looks at me and I walk
away. I walk towards another room and I look in only to see a naked,
older man standing looking at me. His penis is about a foot wide and
reaching all the way to the floor. I am sickened by what I see and I
walk away. I find a door leading outside and I quickly exit. This area
is gated off and I realize there is no escape. I hide behind a barrel
and hope they don't find me. I wake up.

This dream really disturbed me. Am I losing my mind? Am I
to become one of "those" people? I pray that I don't.

February 6, 2007

Another therapy session; and more anxiety about going. Of
course Wayne has to take me. I feel bad that he has to wait in the
truck for an hour while I am in my session but I can't drive by myself
yet. He understands and doesn't complain.

I show Karen my assignment that she gave me from my last
session. She is happy that I did it.

Today Karen wants me to make a Treasure Map which is a
visual representation of those things I want most at this time in my
life, people, opportunities, money, material objects, or experiences
that are fun or challenge me to grow. The images can represent a
particular value that's important to me or can reflect a quality I intend

to develop like courage or patience. This will challenge me to think seriously about what I want at this time in my life. She tells me this gives the soul an opportunity to speak to me through images, without my head getting in the way. The idea is that this Treasure Map will become a vivid demonstration of magnetic energy—the ability to actually draw toward my dreams, goals, and desires, using the power of my imagination. She tells me that I can use pictures or words.

Over the next few days I gather all my magazines and begin my assignment. I find myself drawn toward words that represent the negativity I have been feeling. I also see words that represent what I would like to be in my life. I decided to make two maps.

The first one represents how I feel at this time in my life. **STRUGGLE, LOST, MADNESS, SURVIVE, DISAPPEAR, RUNAWAY, HELP, PANIC ATTACKS, HEART ATTACK, STROKE, DEATH, EVERY DAY I STRUGGLE, STRESS, LOSING CONTROL, AND "YOU DON'T KNOW WHAT'S INSIDE."**

The second map represented what I would like to achieve: **MY LIFE, FREEDOM IS POWER, SUCCESS, CONIFIDENCE, A WRITER, A LITTLE CAFÉ, and LESS FAT.**

February 7, 2007

Today I had to take Kristen for a doctor appointment because she was sick. I got an appointment for early afternoon. I would have time to go to her appointment and make my doctor appointment by 2:00.

Wayne and I took the girls and he sat with us in the waiting room. I thought I would be able to go into the exam room with them without Wayne.

I was fine while the nurse was in the exam room but a few minutes later I felt cold and clammy. My mind was telling me that my sugar was dropping even though I just ate and something was wrong with me. I took a sip of my juice that I packed. (I can't leave the house anymore without my drink and snack. I have to make sure at all time that I have access to my drink in case I need to take my Xanax. I carry a snack with me at all times because I fear that I will have another blood sugar drop like last time.) I calm down and start to feel better.

We leave and go to my doctor's appointment. I tell Wayne that I want to go in by myself. I have yet to be able to do that since anxiety has taken over.

As I'm sitting in the waiting room I can feel the anxiety lurking. I was hoping to see Nurse Lori yet another nurse called me in. Because I don't know her I instantly feel the panic rising.

We go into the exam room and the anxiety intensifies. My heart starts racing and I feel like I'm going to pass out. I start to feel cold and clammy again.

The nurse checks my sugar level and it's normal. I had just

eaten a half of a peanut butter sandwich on the way here so I know I can't be feeling this way because of hunger.

I decide to take the Xanax and ask the nurse if she can revive me if I pass out. She insists that she can.

When the doctor comes in I am shaking hysterically. He talks to me and assures me that the panic attack will not cause me to pass out or die. I am mad that I am sitting in the office having a panic attack. I had been taking baby steps to slowly getting better. After about ten minutes the Xanax starts to work and I feel myself relax.

I told my doctor about what happened last Thursday night. I was convinced that the medication was responsible for causing my blood sugar to drop. He insists that is not the case. I had waited too long to eat. When I started getting shaky from the hunger my mind automatically told me that the Prozac was causing something to be wrong with me. My anxiety magnified my symptoms which then caused the panic attack that night.

He felt that my fear brought that on the same as it did today. I feel that he doesn't think the Prozac is working for me. It is. I wasn't able to tell him that he has helped me immensely. I'm so consumed by the anxiety that I never thanked him.

I tell him that I don't think I will be able to go back to work. He asks me if I think I will ever be able to go back to work. I say, "I don't know." He sees that I am not ready at this time to go back to work tomorrow so he gives me off until March 1st.

Broken Inside…

Although I am happy about that I feel incompetent because I can't go to work like everyone else. I still can't drive by myself. I haven't driven by myself since Christmas time. I haven't been able to go anywhere without Wayne until now.

Also, my doctor wants me to go get a sugar test done at the lab. One that involves me drinking a sugar solution and having my blood sugar tested. There is no way I can go have this done. I have anxiety about drinking the solution and then having to be tested an hour later. I don't think I would be able to wait there an hour. I will have to do that later on in the future. For now I just have to tell myself that my sugar level is fine. I will be careful about what I eat and how often I eat from now on.

February 16, 2007

My mom went with me to my therapy appointment today. I didn't want to go alone. I told her she could just sit in the waiting room but I really wanted her to go in with me. Once we were there I asked her if she wanted to come in with me. She did. I wanted her to tell my therapist from her viewpoint how my disorder had altered my life.

I am always worried about what people think of me and I wanted Karen to know that this disorder has changed me. We also went over the dynamics of our family. My mom told her that my great grandfather had been a little mental. Maybe that's where I get it from.

After my session my mom and I went to Cato. I told her that I wanted to buy some clothes but I wouldn't be able to try them on in the store. I feared that I would have a panic attack in the dressing room in the middle of getting dressed.

I walked into the store with my mom. I grabbed all the clothes that I liked and thought would fit and walked straight to the counter.

As the sales associate rang up my items I thought, "What if I have a panic attack in the middle of her ringing up my items"? I tried to push the thought away and concentrate on other things.

I told my mom that once I was done paying for my items I would go sit in the car. I told her I would be fine I just didn't want to stay in the store any longer than I had to.

As I was sitting in the car I felt guilty about buying myself clothes when I wasn't even working but I needed them just the same.

Later I had to rest because I was tired from everything I had done today.

February 21, 2007

Tonight Wayne and I have to go to Kristen's school for a Driver's Ed Parent Orientation meeting. It's scheduled at 7pm. We go and I sit in the back row of the auditorium which is located near the entrance to the school. I know that my truck is not far from the door in case I need to make an escape. I was able to sit through the hour long seminar. I was even able to get up and walk Kayli to the bathroom. I felt proud that I was able to do something involving my daughter. It was a good day.

February 25, 2007

I am supposed to be going back to work this Thursday. I am terrified. Wayne got the news last week that he will be going back to work soon. I know that eventually I will have to get up with Kayli in the morning by myself and have to take her to school and pick her up by myself. Even though I haven't been able to do that yet by myself and haven't been able to since Christmas time I know that it's something I will be expected to do.

I don't think I will be able to go back to my job. I am afraid of being there for seven hours. I'm worried that I will have a panic attack or feel anxiety coming on and I won't be able to escape. It's not fair for me to work in a school and know that I can no longer be responsible for the kids that I worked with.

To date I haven't been able to handle anything that involves me being somewhere for more than four hours. What if I can't handle the seven hour workday five days a week? I still require a nap some days. I can't just pop a Xanax at work when I feel the anxiety coming on. The medicine makes me drowsy. Right now I have to have my Xanax, a drink, and a snack with me at all times. I won't be able to do that at my job. I can't tell the people that I work with what I'm going through. I don't want people to think I'm crazy or feel that I have an imaginary illness. I'm afraid if I talk to them about it I may actually have a panic attack just thinking about it. I know my coworkers care about me and I miss the children but I am not the same person I was. I've lost my independence and am struggling to get that back. Each day I take baby steps to get better. I appreciate any little thing I can do now. The anxiety has crippled me to the point that I can no longer function like I used to. I deal with that everyday.

I am contemplating giving my resignation letter to work tomorrow. I feel immense guilt about that.

February 28, 2007

Today I had therapy with Karen. I look forward to therapy now. I was happy to share with her some of my accomplishments since our last session.

What I found out today scares me. These last couple sessions I talk and talk and now I have to start the work. I don't want to because I am scared. She gave me some literature on Conquering Anxiety. She wanted me to read it when I got home.

I told her that I am scared about going back to work on Thursday because I didn't feel I was ready. I ask her if it's wrong that I put myself first and her answer, "No." I told her I thought I would just email the principal and tell her I wouldn't be returning to work. I didn't want to have to face her. I also didn't feel it was fair to keep them waiting on me. I knew I wasn't capable of going back to work. Karen didn't think that was the mature thing to do. Instead of emailing my work it was better to just call and talk to them. I dreaded that.

When I went home I did call the principal and tell her I wouldn't be returning to work. She instructed me to call the district office and I did. I left a message with them. I decided to contact the Hartford concerning extending my disability. Once my doctor and therapist filled out the appropriate paperwork they would make their decision.

I started to read the information Karen gave me on Conquering Anxiety. This information came from the website www.conqueringanxiety.com. There are 12 chapters. Chapter One is the introduction. Chapter Twelve is the conclusion.

Chapter Two lists the seven keys to overcoming anxiety: Educate Yourself, Address Roadblocks, Set Gradual, Progressive Goals, Train Your Body and Mind to Respond to Stress Differently, Make Wellness a Way of Life, Personalize Your Solution, and Celebrate Your Successes.

Chapter Three discusses how the first key of overcoming anxiety is educating yourself. Learn what anxiety is, how it affects you, and the scientific reasons for your symptoms. They state that anxiety is a real, treatable illness. They go on to say that "one in every eight Americans suffers from overwhelming anxiety and fear

that disrupts their daily lives, referred to as an anxiety disorder."
Understanding what happens to your body when you feel anxious is
understanding how the brain works.

The fight or flight response is your body's automatic, inborn
response that protects your survival. It prepares the body to "fight" or
"flee" from any real or perceived threat to your survival.
When the fight or flight response occurs, it stimulates an area of your
brain called the hypothalamus. The hypothalamus prepares your body
for fighting or running. It does this by flooding your brain with
chemicals such as adrenaline, noradrenaline, and coritsol. This
process is what creates the physical reactions of a panic attack.

Anxiety follows a cycle that consists of five phases: Trigger,
Fight or Flight, Internalizing, Assuming the Worst, and Increase or
Intensification of Symptoms.

Chapter Four discusses addressing roadblocks. They are:
fear of change, feel lack of time or energy, feeling not good enough,
doubting the power within, and lacking skills and inner resources.

Chapter Five: Set Gradual, Progressive Goals. The process
of conquering anxiety requires at least a tiny part of you to accept the
possibility that you have the power within to succeed.

Chapter Six: Train your body and mind to respond to stress
differently. The key to conquering anxiety is knowledge and
consistently applying anxiety-reducing techniques in your daily life
by improving your external environment and changing your internal

Broken Inside…

environment.

Chapter Seven discusses how to learn deep breathing. This involves deliberately learning to slow your breathing rate and breathe from the diaphragm.

Chapter Eight: How to overcome your fear of losing control. This is one of my biggest problems. I always have to be in control. I've always had to control every aspect of my life and felt I needed to control how others acted around me. What this article discusses is it doesn't matter that I don't have complete control over my external environment instead I have to learn how I react to life's events. This is more important than trying to control life's events. You determine your happiness by controlling your internal environment, not your external one. If you control how you react to life's events, you control your reality. This makes sense to me.

Chapter Nine: Make wellness a way of life, Chapter Ten: Personalize your solution, and Chapter Eleven: Celebrate your successes are self explanatory.

I make it a point to incorporate these strategies into my daily life now.

March 2, 2007

I am so proud of myself. Today for the first time in two months I was able to drive Kayli to school without Wayne or my mom with me. I knew if I needed to I could call Wayne and have him come get me if anything happened to me. I had my mom's cell phone. My sister's car was parked at our house while she was in California and she left the keys in case we needed to move it. What an accomplishment to be dressed and out the door to take my daughter to school. I wasn't even nervous after dropping her off knowing I'd be in the truck by myself. I made the trip home. Today accomplished a goal. It was a good day.

March 3, 2007

Today was Heather's Birthday Party. We decided to have it at my house since I'm not able to go out to lunch or dinner like we normally do. I am not able to sit in a restaurant to eat. I knew I wouldn't be able to go to the movies or bowling if Heather wanted to. She decided that we were going to have a Mary Kay party at my house.

I was having a great anxiety-free day until the lady never showed up. I had called her a few times and she never returned my calls. It really bothered me because this stressed me out. My mom kept telling me to calm down; that it was okay. My sister told me it wasn't my fault so I tried to let it go. It still bothers me that I couldn't fix this problem. We went ahead and celebrated without having the Mary Kay party.

Broken Inside…

March 4, 2007

I was able to drive Heather to Laurie's house to have her consultation for her hair. It was only about five miles from my house. While we were there getting Heather's consultation I decided to get my hair cut. I hoped I wouldn't have a panic attack in the middle of getting my hair cut. Thank God I didn't. I am proud of myself today.

March 6, 2007

Wayne started his new job today. I had to drive Kayli to school by myself. I was able to do it. After dropping her off I drove the back roads home. Once I got home I relaxed. I had my mom go with me to pick her up because it took a lot for me to go by myself this morning.

March 7, 2007

I am really stressing about tomorrow. I have to take my mom to work at 8am then drop Kayli off by 8:30, go to therapy, and drive home by myself. I have to pick Kayli up from school then pick my mom up at 5:00 after that it's my turn to carpool. I have to drive to Dover to pick Lauren up and then drive the girls to practice in Middletown by myself. I am really scared to be alone while driving the girls to practice because if I have a panic attack in the car I won't have anyone to drive for me. I don't want to have to ask Karen or Keesha to switch days with me. I tell myself I can do it.

March 8, 2007

This morning I had to take Kayli to school at 8:30 am by myself. I had a 9:30 am appointment with my therapist for my counseling. I dropped Kayli off and told myself I could drive to my appointment in Dover a few miles away from her school.

When I got there I couldn't park out front so I had to park in the parking lot and walk up the steps.

By the time I walked down the long hall to the office my heart was racing which was fine because I told myself it was racing because I did a lot of walking. I decided that I would go right to my appointment and just wait in the waiting room until my appointment time.

I had my session all mapped out in my mind. Last session Karen talked about me not just talking during the session but that I needed to start doing the "work." That bothered me because I didn't feel ready to do the "work" part of my session. I wanted to talk about us doing that in a later session because I wanted to know exactly what we would be working on and I was going to take notes. That way at home I could start the work where I felt safe.

As I was sitting in the waiting room trying to read a magazine I started to feel the anxiety. I told myself I would be ok and to calm down. Then I started to feel clammy, my heart started racing, and I got scared. I realized at that moment I had no "safety net." Wayne wasn't out in the truck waiting for me like he's done all my other sessions. I knew that I was there all alone and I would have to drive myself home.

I walked over and told the secretary that I was getting ready to have a panic attack. For a spilt second I had the urge to run and get out of there but I knew I couldn't. I immediately sat down and took half of my Xanax. I started to cry. I told the secretary that I had just dropped my daughter off at school and I drove there by myself which is something I haven't done yet.

The secretary knocked on Karen's door while she was in the middle of a session with another patient to tell her I was having a panic attack. Karen came out of the office to ask me what was wrong. I told her I was having a panic attack and that I just took my medication to help calm me down. She wanted me to relax and practice deep breathing while she finished up with her session. I had to wait in the waiting room for about twenty minutes until her session was finished.

After awhile my medication started to work and I could feel myself relaxing some. I called my sister Tara to see if she could have her friend Tim drive her to my therapist's office and she could drive me home and Tim could drive my mom's car home. She wasn't home so I left her a message on her cell phone.

I then called my sister Heather. I was crying. I told her what happened. I told her to keep trying to reach Tara so she could pick me up. She told me I would be fine.

Broken Inside…

It was then time for my session. I was still shaking and crying when I went into her office. I told Karen all the things I had planned to do today. I knew that I wouldn't be able to drive the girls to practice tonight. She said that last night when I knew I wouldn't be able to do all these things I didn't acknowledge how that made me feel; scared.

I asked her if we could turn off the lights in the room because they were bothering my eyes. I crossed my arms and leaned back on the couch. She had me practice deep breathing.

She asked me to picture in my mind a memory I had of me as a child. The one I chose was that of me standing next to my father when he kicked my mom out of the house. To date I have never associated any feelings with this memory. She wanted me to freeze that image in my mind and talk to that little girl.

In my mind I walked over to her and comforted her. I talked to her as if I were talking to my own daughter. I felt her fear. I embraced her and told her I understood her pain. At that moment I realized that I never acknowledged my feelings, whether consciously or not. I must've repressed my feelings when I was a child. I know that my father was an alcoholic who abused my mother for the last three of their seven years of marriage. There were times that my father didn't provide for us and we went without food. My mom did everything she could to take care of us. On some level I must've never felt nurtured and the idea of asking for help was wrong. Maybe it wasn't something I was taught was ok to do. This may be why I cannot be around people when I am having a panic attack. In my mind I'm not supposed to ask for help.

Karen stated that each of us has an "inner child." I never heard of the "inner child" and didn't know I had one. I do know that I have been repressing something and I don't want to face it because then I have to face all the feelings that go along with it.

Karen instructed me to embrace my "inner child." I had told her that whenever I feel anxiety coming on I tell myself, "Stop it." Instead I am to tell myself that I will be ok. This was a good session even though it didn't go as I planned. In some small way I feel that my "inner child" wanted to be acknowledged and heard.

In the meantime Tara called to tell me she was not able to pick me up from my session. I drove myself home still a little nervous.

I called Karen (Lauren's mom) and she wasn't home. I didn't leave a message. I didn't want to ask her to have to drive tonight because I would have to drive the kids to north Dover. I knew I wouldn't be able to drive by myself.

Instead I called Keesha and left a message on her cell phone. I called Martha to see if she could pick Kayli up from school. She wasn't able to.

Tara called to tell me that she was coming down later to get her car. I asked her if she could pick Kayli up from school on her way to my house. She said she would. Thank God for sisters. I hung up the phone and took a two hour nap. I was mentally drained.

Later that afternoon, I called Keesha to tell her I couldn't drive tonight because I was sick. That wasn't exactly a lie. I couldn't very well tell her what was really wrong with me. I didn't feel that I could tell Karen or Keesha what was really wrong with me because these are two of the nicest, most normal women I knew and I didn't want them to think I was mentally ill. I was afraid that they wouldn't trust me with their kids. Keesha said that she could drive. When Keesha drives she picks Kayli up at the house so I didn't have to worry about driving to north Dover. Feeling relieved I hung up the phone and took another nap.

March 9, 2007

Kristen missed the bus this morning so I figured I would drop her off on the way to take my mom to work. After that I would drop Kayli off at school and drive back by myself.

I didn't think much about that but when it came time to actually leave the house I felt the panic attack come on. I felt clammy, scared, and my heart started racing. For a brief moment I thought I wouldn't be able to leave the house. I told my mom I was feeling the panic attack coming on.

She told me that I would be ok. She said that I could drop Kristen off and then drop her off. If I wasn't able to drive Kayli to school we could just come home.

Broken Inside...

Kristen told me to stop worrying about having the panic attack because worrying about it was causing me to have one. Instantly I felt the panic lessen and I actually walked out the front door and drove Kristen to school which is only about a mile from my house.

Next I drove the couple miles from there to my mom's work. After I dropped her off I had to keep reminding myself that I would be ok driving. I really wanted to be able to take Kayli to school. I didn't want her to miss a day of school because I wasn't able to drive by myself. I thought that I could do this. When I got closer to my house I realized that I would be able to take her to school. From my house her school is about ten miles or so. As I was driving I kept telling myself, "I'm stronger today." "I didn't have the panic attack." "I didn't have to take a Xanax *and* I was able to drive by myself." Once I dropped her off I drove the back roads home.

I came home and felt that I accomplished a lot. I took a nap because I needed to rest my mind. When it was time to pick Kayli up from school I was able to.

That evening I even drove to my mom's work by myself and picked her up. We then went to the dollar store. I shopped a little. I did all this without feeling any anxiety. Maybe I am stronger.

March 10, 2007

Today Kristen and Kayli had a competition at the Baltimore Convention Center in Baltimore, Maryland. My goal for today was to be able to go to the competition without having to take a Xanax. We had a two hour drive from my house. I felt calm about today because Wayne was driving and I knew I had mastered going to the last few competitions. I told myself if I needed the medication I would take it. I wasn't going to beat myself up about that.

After about an hour of driving the panic thoughts started to come. I kept thinking, "What if I have a panic attack in the truck"? If I did I wouldn't be able to go in the convention center. I would have to sit in the truck for five hours by myself. I kept trying to push the thought out of my head. Then I thought, "What if I have a panic attack while I'm in the convention center?"

It was then that I decided I had to take the medication. After a little while I started to calm down and the thoughts went away. I was able to go the competition which lasted about five hours.

Where I sat I kept reminding myself where the door was. I could see outside and I knew my truck was only a block away if I needed to make an escape. As the competition wore on I was even able to walk around a little and talk to some of the parents. I'm glad I got through this day. By the end of the night I was completely exhausted.

That night my sister spent the night because she came down to get her hair done. She was loaning me her other car so I wouldn't have to take my mom back and forth to work. That night after everyone went to sleep I told her about my recent panic attacks and how I felt I was getting stronger. She agreed with me. She reminded me how a few weeks ago I saw the panic attacks as the problem. Now I was able to see that the panic attacks are brought on by my stress, worry, and fear. If I'm able to conquer those maybe then I can learn how to control the panic attacks. She also said that the stress, worry, and fear brought on the panic attacks and the fear of them is what caused the agoraphobia. I finally understood how I got to this point in my life. Eventually I would like to be medication free but for now I know I need it and that's ok.

March 13, 2007

Last night I dreamt that *I was visiting my work. I walked into the classroom I work in and saw that there were two substitutes' one for me and one for Amy. Amy told me that she was going out to lunch so they hired a substitute for her. She then told me that since the school hired a long-term substitute for me that they have a right to know what's wrong with me. I didn't want to have to tell her what was wrong with me. Instead of answering her I asked if I could see the kids. They were napping so I was able to peek in on them. The next thing I'm walking through the school and looking into the different classrooms. No one noticed that I was there which was fine with me. I was able to blend in.*

When I woke up the next morning I felt guilty about having taken off work all this time. I know that I need time to get myself together but now I feel like I should've been able to go to work after all. I was able to drop Kayli off at school and pick her up from school all by myself. This is progress for me.

Tonight is Karen's turn to drive. I know I have to drop Mariah and Kayli off to her at the skating rink in Dover. I'm a little nervous about that. I tell myself not to worry about that. When the time comes to leave the house I will be fine. I was able to drop them off but I had to take the back roads home since the skating rink is out of my "safety zone."

March 14, 2007

I did something today that I haven't been able to do for two months. After I dropped Kayli off at school I drove the back roads to Witt Brothers Market to get some groceries. I told myself that if I felt anxiety on the way there I would simply drive past the store and go home.

Once I got there I felt no anxiety. I walked around the little market and gathered a few items. I didn't feel anxiety but I didn't want to be in there very long so I hurried.

As I walked out of the store I was very proud of myself. I accomplished this goal today. I took the back roads home and enjoyed the warm day.

Broken Inside…

March 15, 2007

Tonight while I was reading the newspaper I came across an article that talked about Camp Barnes which is an overnight camp that's held during the summer. It's sponsored through the Police Athletic League. I was really excited about sending Kayli there this summer. My nephew went last year and he had a really good time. The camp is open for three separate weeks in the summer for boys and three separate weeks for girls. At the end of the article the last thing it said was that there was a state trooper at the camp at all times.

My immediate thought was that "they" were molesting the kids. I don't know why I thought this. I know it sounds stupid. Maybe I was worried about a male police officer being with the kids. I didn't think about the fact that there could be a female officer there. Anyway I brushed the thought off.

March 16, 2007

After dropping Kayli off at school today I went to the State Police Headquarters to pick up the applications for Camp Barnes. I remember sitting at the red light and I had this little gut feeling in the pit of my stomach that told me not to go to police department. I shrugged it off and continued driving there.

I remembered that I would have to walk up the steps to the front door. The idea of me having to walk up the steps in my mind meant that my heart racing would trigger a panic attack. I told myself I would be fine.

While I was waiting to get the applications from the officer there was another person talking to the officer so I had to wait. I was standing there and I was looking at the police officer and instantly I felt the panic attack coming on. I felt my skin getting clammy and my arms and vagina going numb. Looking at him I felt like he would know that I would need help since he was someone to go to when you need help. I calmly turned around and left the building.

I got into the car and my heart was racing by this time. I talked to myself out loud all the way home. I kept telling myself I was fine. I grabbed my bottle of Xanax and reminded myself that I could take one if I needed it. I took deep breaths to relax myself.

When I got home I lay down and took a nap. That afternoon I was thinking about having to pick Kayli up from school. When I did I felt the panic attack come on. I told myself I wasn't going to pick her up so I called my friend Martha. She told me she would pick Kayli up for me. Feeling relieved that I didn't have to go anywhere I laid back down and relaxed until Kayli came home from school. I told Kristen and Kayli that I wasn't feeling well because I knew I wouldn't be able to do anything the rest of the night.

March 22, 2007

I had my first psychiatry appointment today. I scheduled it in the morning so that my mom could go with me. I was afraid that I would have a panic attack in the psychiatrist's office since I had one at my last therapy session. I was calm until I got there.

Once in the waiting room I was given a package of forms to fill out. I felt the anxiety come on. I started to feel clammy and my heart was racing. I talked to myself telling myself that the only reason I was feeling the panic attack coming on was that I was afraid I was going to have one and I was afraid of seeing this psychiatrist. I was able to calm myself down and I didn't have a panic attack.

When I first got into the psychiatrist's office I told her why I was there and that the Hartford would be contacting her regarding my short-term disability. I told her I realized that she would have to talk to them only after seeing me one session.

She asked me a lot of questions about me and my family. I liked that she asked questions and took notes. During this short time of about 50 minutes I tried to cram my whole life story in and because of this I was talking fast. I was nervous, too so that also explained why I was talking fast. I had told her about the anxiety, panic attacks, agoraphobia, depression, feeling like I was going crazy and she proceeds to tell me that she believes I suffer from bi-polar disorder because of my episodes of depression, racing thoughts (which are my panic thoughts), and rapid speech. I told her that even though she's the doctor I do not agree with her diagnosis. Maybe I am wrong but I don't know how she thinks she can meet me and in five minutes diagnose me with something I don't believe I have.

We changed the subject to my current medications. She tells me which meds I can take if I want to switch meds. I tell her that I don't want to switch meds and I asked her if I have to because if I do that will only cause a whole new set of anxiety stressors for me. She tells me that I don't. I am relieved. She believes the medications I am taking are the right medications for me.

We end the session and I am glad I made it through. I already had my next appointment scheduled so I went out to the car.

I took my mom to work and went home. I was mentally drained from my session so I took a two hour nap. I got some housework done when I woke up. I then cooked dinner and picked Kayli up from school.

Since it was my turn to shuttle the girls to Karen I dropped Kayli and Mariah off to Karen and then took Kristen to drop off some papers to Killen's Pond for her new job, then we went to pick my mom up from work. When I got home I was totally exhausted. I ate dinner and watched television until it was time to pick Kayli up from Karen after their practice that night.

Wayne came home from work and asked me how my session went and did I go. I told him that yes I went and it went fine.

Broken Inside…

He went with me to pick Kayli and Mariah up because I was so tired I could barely function. I asked him if it was bad for me to have to take naps during the day when I need it. It made me feel good that he said, "No."

March 23, 2007

I accomplished a goal today. If nothing else my goal was to get through my therapy session without having a panic attack since the last time I had therapy I had a panic attack. I tried not to think of my appointment this morning. I got up and got Kayli up for school. After I dropped her off at school I stopped to get gas.

While I was driving I kept talking to myself saying things like, "On Tuesday I drove all the way to and from Middletown by myself and sat at practice for two hours and I was fine." "I need to go to therapy because it's helping me." "Therapy didn't cause my anxiety attack." "If I have an anxiety attack there I will take my Xanax and I will be fine." "Today the only thing I have to do is get through therapy and after that I can relax the rest of the day."

When I got to therapy I did not feel any anxiety. Sitting in Karen's office I told her my goal for today was to get through therapy without an anxiety attack. I managed to do that. She feels I am making some progress.

Broken Inside…

March 25, 2007

I was able to go to La Fontana in Magnolia with Wayne, Kristen, Kayli, Heather, Lee, Anthony, Lexi, Tara, and my mom. It was so nice to be able to eat in a restaurant. When we first got there it was empty. After awhile other people were seated near us. I kept telling myself I would be ok. I made it through my entire meal and rejoiced at being able to get through this.

Later at home my mom asked me to call to have a snack gift basket delivered to Kristen that would be from both of us. I thought that sounded like a great idea. Out of nowhere this idea came to me. Why not make cheerleader gift baskets and sell them at the cheerleading competitions?

I visualized myself sitting at the vendor tables with my baskets. I wasn't sure how I could do it but I sat down and wrote a plan. I knew I would have many phone calls to make and I was up for the challenge. I had remembered Karen asking me what had happened to my idea about my mom, sisters, and I opening a Café. I explained to her that with our credit, financial situations, and the fact that my sister Tara was planning to move to California, we squashed that. Not to mention the fact that none of us knew the first thing about the restaurant business. My idea about the cheerleader gift baskets seemed attainable.

Broken Inside…

March 26, 2007

I was excited when I woke up this morning. I had a future plan. First I visualized the product. I wanted to make the baskets for youth age, junior age, and teens. I would fill them with cheerleader accessories and gift wrap them. I thought a coach's basket sounded like a good idea as well.

I went on-line and found out there weren't many cheerleader gift baskets at the websites that I went to. The ones that had them weren't what I pictured mine to be. I then typed in "cheerleader accessories" to get an idea of what products I felt the girls would like. I wrote a list of the items I wanted to fill the baskets with. I wrote the names of the websites and prices down. Next, I had to figure out, "Do I get permission from the arena or the cheerleading company who sponsors the event?"

I made a few calls to different arenas and convention centers. I found out that I had to go through the cheerleading companies. I got all of the program guides from last year to get a list of the cheerleading companies and their phone numbers. I called a few. Some of them do not allow outside vendors. The ones that I contacted that did were very excited about my idea. These companies would send me their competition schedules and I could pick and choose which events to attend. As a parent of all-star cheerleaders I have never been to an event where someone has sold cheerleader gift baskets.

Broken Inside…

I also contacted the Division of Revenue to find out how to apply for a business license. I also called the Delaware Small Business Development Center and was given information on the "Start your business right" seminar. This wasn't required but I thought I would attend this when I could.

I wrote all the information down so I could visualize my plan. I sat back and thought about how this would benefit me. I could create something, have fun while I was doing it, work at my own pace, and choose when and where I could work. I wouldn't have to be by myself because my mom and daughters offered to help me work at the competitions.

I decided to create a website so I could begin to sell the gift baskets on-line.

I realized that I would not be able to go back to Charlton. There is a part of me that is a changed person since these last three months. I am not the same person I was and I don't feel confident that I can do my job there. I don't want to be responsible for the kids. I don't feel that it's fair that I may not be able to do my job because of my anxiety. I was so excited to have something else to look forward to.

March 27, 2007

Last night I dreamt that *I was lying on my bed with my head at the bottom of the bed. There was a person laying to the right of me.*

Broken Inside…

The next thing that happens is a hand comes walking up my back. I woke up screaming.

This morning I watched the DVD version of "The Secret" that Karen had given me at my last session. I had no idea what it was about. I was instantly intrigued by the messages.

The messages I got out of it were, thoughts become things, what you think about you bring about, whatever thought in your life has done can be undone, attitude gratitude, believe you can have what you want and believe you deserve it, whatever the mind can believe it can achieve, focus on what you want, not want you don't, we are creators of our own universe, as you love yourself you'll love others, it's not your job to change the people around you, all power is from within and it is under our control, inner happiness is the fuel of success, what do I choose to do now; live in the past or live in the future, your life will be what you create it as. I read these messages to myself everyday because I believe for me they are simple, yet powerful words of wisdom.

I wrote down all of the messages I felt were vital for me. I typed it up and am sending a copy to my two sisters. I have it on my refrigerator so I can refer back to it on a daily basis.

I spent the afternoon working on designing my website. I felt overwhelmed because I did not envision what I wanted it to look like. I did come up with a name for my company. In order to post pictures of the baskets I would have to make them first. I liked the idea that I could purchase the baskets and the items a little at a time so that I wouldn't have to put a lot of money out all at once.

I wouldn't dare ask for a loan because I don't have great credit. Later that night, I started to feel depressed about creating the website because maybe I should've waited on that. Then I started to think that maybe I shouldn't go ahead with my idea. I started to doubt myself. I told myself that I have bad credit, I pay my bills late, I don't have a lot of money, and yet I'm going to run a company. What do I know about running my own business? Am I going to be able to pay my own taxes? Can I market my product?

When I went to bed I lay there thinking I am bi-polar because my gift basket idea was the "high" and the depression I was feeling was the "low." I became more depressed because I believed the psychiatrist was right, "I do have bi-polar." I got on-line and looked up the symptoms for bi-polar. I do have some of the "manic" such as racing thoughts, fast speech and some of the "depression" factor. I went to sleep feeling like a failure.

March 28, 2007

Last night I dreamt that *my mom caught a male friend of hers having sex with a child and that she knew about it and she didn't do anything about it. I confronted her about it in the dream by telling her that his wife had a right to know what he did. She did not agree with me and we argued.* The dream ends. What does this mean?

Broken Inside…

While lying in bed this morning I thought about my cheerleading gift basket business. I thought that once I made the baskets I could take a picture of my girls in their cheerleading uniforms with the gift baskets. Happy that I had a picture of how I wanted the website to look I felt better.

I remembered talking to Karen about that side of me that I constantly battle. The side that tells me I can't do something because I am nobody and I'm worthless. We had talked about this being that child-like part of myself. As a child I felt these feelings at some point.

What I realized today was that I felt the way I did last night because I am scared. I was aware and acknowledged this feeling. I accepted it and understood why I felt this way. I am scared that I don't deserve my own company because I am a bad person. I am scared that I will try and fail. I am afraid of the unknown but more than that I am afraid of success and happiness because for me that represents the end of my life.

It dawned on me that I intentionally, subconsciously self-destruct because I am afraid to change who I am. I feel comfortable holding onto fear because I don't know how to let it go. It's what I'm used to doing. I've always equated happiness with death. I sense that someone has taken my happiness from me and in essence killed a part of me. I think that's the part of me that feels I don't deserve anything. This is where my low self-esteem and low self-worth stem from.

Broken Inside…

Today I watched the DVD "The Sedona Method" self-esteem on success. It talks about letting go of uncomfortable emotions, thoughts, and feelings. Another method talks about visualizing what you want, believing you deserve it, and letting go of the negative thoughts, feelings, and emotions that keep you from what you visualize. This was profound to me.

I understand that I've been listening to these negative thoughts for so long that I couldn't achieve any success in my life. Today I was able to let go of being afraid and visualized me running this business. I want to continue working toward my goal. Even if it doesn't work out at least I tried. As I did with "The Secret" I took notes while watching "The Sedona Method" and typed it up. I am sending a copy of this to my sisters as well. I am keeping a copy of this on my refrigerator too so I can refer back to it.

March 30, 2007

I needed to run some errands today to get prepared for our trip to Florida. I decided that we would go to the mall when it first opened. I told Kayli that I thought I would be ok to walk into Old Navy and if nothing else I could leave the mall as soon as we were done shopping in Old Navy.

I told Kristen that she could take her time shopping and when she was done she could meet me in the truck. I would wait for her there. I decided to go to J.C. Penny's first because my mom gave me a gift card for Kayli.

I parked at the entrance right by the young girls clothing section. I knew I could zip in and get what we needed and leave quickly. I thought I would be ok because I would be near the door.

Once inside I was fine. I was even able to sit in the waiting room with Kayli while she tried clothes on. She still wanted to go to Old Navy and I thought I could do it because Old Navy is right outside of J.C. Penney in the mall. I told myself over and over again I would be fine. Besides I have been to the mall many times before and never had anxiety about going. I was fine until I exited J.C. Penney and entered the mall.

This feeling came over me of total fear. I felt the mall closing in on me. I told myself I could do this. We continued on walking toward Old Navy. As I walked further into the store I felt the beginning of a panic attack coming on. At that moment I realized I could not escape quickly if I needed to. There weren't any doors nearby. I turned around and told Kayli we had to leave.

I started walking toward the mall to escape. Kayli asked me what was wrong. I told her I was going to have a panic attack and that I needed to leave. She said to me, "You're going to be ok mom." I needed to hear that. The panic started to slowly subside and I was able to walk around the store a little. We didn't find what we were looking for and so we went back to J.C.Penney. I knew I would be ok once I got there because the door was nearby. We shopped for a little while and then went out to the truck.

I drove to where I would meet Kristen and relaxed while waiting for her. I was happy that I was able to conquer this and I did it without having to take a Xanax.

March 31, 2007

The kids had a competition in Ocean City, MD today. We drove to Wayne's parents to pick them up so they could ride with us to the competition. Wayne's brother, Bob also went with us. It was the first time he'd ever been to any of their competitions. I felt very calm today because we went to this arena last year. I told myself that if I felt any anxiety I would take the Xanax. I was able to go to this competition without taking a Xanax. This is progress for me. I was able to see the exit doors from where I sat and I knew my truck wasn' far from the doors. I was even able to walk around the vendors. I wanted to get an idea of what other people were selling.

After the competition we spent the night at his parent's house because we had to be back at the competition the next day for their second competition. I was a little nervous about going there since I haven't been there since post-panic disorder. We got back to their house in time to go to sleep. The next morning I worried about having to sit at their house all day until we had to leave for Ocean City. Wayne left to take his brother to Georgetown.

Broken Inside…

Wayne's mom and I decided to ride out to the Rehoboth Outlets. About halfway there I started to panic because I realized that I was by myself with her and I didn't want to have a panic attack in front of her. I kept reminding myself that I was ok and that I had went out plenty of times with her before my disorder. I was able to go into two stores. I went in, got what I needed, and left the store. I was fine because I wasn't in there long and I was near the door.

After we left the outlets we drove for about thirty minutes to Millsboro to Rose's Department Store. I had to keep reminding myself I would be ok. We weren't in Rose's long.

Mentally exhausted I was finally able to relax in the car on the way back to her house. The rest of the day I kept my mind busy by reading.

When it was time to go to the competition I was feeling no anxiety. Wayne was with us and I was able to go without a Xanax. I was very glad to make it through this weekend.

April 2, 2007

Not a good day. I was scheduled to have a psychiatrist appointment this morning. I canceled it because I felt I had too much going on with having to pack for Florida. We were leaving at 3 am and I had a lot to do today.

I had written a list of everything that I needed to do and realized I had way too much to do. I started to panic. I began to pack and felt a panic attack coming on. I talked to myself out loud assuring myself I was going to be ok. I knew that I wouldn't be able to get everything done because I was feeling overwhelmed about this trip.

I started to have more of the anxiety so I looked at my list and circled what had to be done and told myself anything else could be done later. I then took a nap to clear my thoughts. I told the kids to leave me alone because I couldn't focus on anything at the moment.

After my nap I felt better. I continued packing and asked my mom to go with me that evening to finish my errands that way I wouldn't have to be by myself. I was able to get most of the things on my list done. It left room for me to be able to have time to clean the house before I left.

April 3, 2007

We woke up at 3 am and were out the door at 3:30 am to drive to Florida. I was nervous about the fifteen hour drive. What if I had a panic attack? What if I couldn't find a hospital nearby? As we were driving I started to feel trapped in the truck where normally I felt safe there. I was scared and wanted to scream and jump out of the truck.

I kept repeating over and over again the words I heard from the Sedona Method CD. "Let it go", "Let it go." I tried really hard to let go of those thoughts. I finally separated those thoughts from my conscious mind and tried to concentrate on the positive things this trip would bring.

Broken Inside…

I started to feel the excitement about going to Florida. I knew the weather there would be nice and I pictured myself sitting there relaxing by the pool. I also knew that these past few months have been extremely mentally exhausting and even though I haven't been at work since December I needed a vacation; a vacation from my mind.

April 9, 2007

What a great vacation. I deserved it. I was anxiety free during the whole trip. I enjoyed the weather. I sat by the pool. I went to the kid's competitions. Life is good.

April 12, 2007

Today I did something I thought I would never do. I went online and submitted my story to the Montel Williams Show website. I felt like because Montel Williams has been suffering with MS since 1999 he knows what it's like to wake up everyday and have to face a disorder. I have watched his show many times and see the passion he has for helping people. I wanted to share my story through his show because I want people to know what it's like to live with an anxiety disorder and I think he would show compassion for my situation. If I hear nothing from the show about appearing that will be ok because at least I tried.

Broken Inside...

April 16, 2007

    I woke up at 6 am this morning after having a dream that really scared me. I had dreamt that *I was in this house with a whole bunch of people. I walked into a room and there was this woman standing in front of a computer. Seated in front of the computer was a young girl with blonde hair. As I walked towards the computer the woman asked if I wanted to watch what they were watching. I looked at the computer and saw that they were watching a porno. I told her "NO" and left the room. A few minutes later I walked into the same room but the room was in darkness. I noticed the curtains were closed. I turned and tried to open the door because I was scared and wanted to leave the room. I kept turning the doorknob and pulling at the door and I couldn't get out. I kept pulling on the door and finally it opened. I went out into the living room/ bedroom area. It was just me and Wayne. We lay down to go to sleep. He was lying behind me. I couldn't see his face. I could only feel his hand resting on my stomach where my belly button was. His other hand was resting on my forehead over my left eye. I wasn't afraid until his hand that was on my stomach began to grab me in such a way that it hurt me. I got scared. I felt his hand pressing on my forehead. I then realized that I heard the shower running. At that moment I realized that the person in the bed with me wasn't Wayne.* I screamed and woke up.

Broken Inside…

Once I realized I was in the bed alone I ran into the bathroom where Wayne was taking a shower. I wasn't able to go back to sleep after that.

April 19, 2007

I've had anxiety since Monday because I had to go to my doctor's appointment today by myself. I had already cancelled my appointment from the other day and rescheduled it for today so I knew I had to go. Wayne reminded me that I needed to go so that I could get my benefits extended. I knew this but I was scared to go by myself.

The last time I went to my doctor's appointment when Wayne drove me I had a panic attack in the exam room and I was worried I would have one today. I was also worried about my blood pressure being a little high. I was afraid if it was that would cause me to have a panic attack in the office and I wouldn't be able to drive myself home.

I thought about letting Kristen stay home from school so she could go with me for fear that I couldn't drive myself home. I decided against that because she had already missed a few days of school from when we went to Florida. Kayli told me she would go with me but she wouldn't be able to drive me home if I couldn't drive. I told her thanks but no thanks. I was really hoping my mom would be able to go with me. She couldn't so I had to face the fact that I had to do this myself.

When I got up this morning I went along as I did every other morning getting Kayli ready for school. I tried not to think about going to the doctor's office. One thing at a time I kept telling myself.

Then the thoughts came. I imagined myself having a panic attack in the doctor's office and being rushed out by ambulance. I had to talk to myself for almost two hours reminding myself that I could do this. I told myself that I was stronger today than the last time I went. I kept battling this in my head. The one side of me telling me something bad would happen and the other side telling me to let go of the negative thoughts and think positive.

After leaving the house I drove Kayli to school. Afterwards I told myself that I was simply going to drive to Milford and if I had anxiety than I would skip the doctor appointment. I had to pick Kayli's physical form up from her doctor's office anyway so I could at least do that.

I got to my doctor's appointment and I was a little shaky. I went in and signed myself in. I sat in the waiting room and continued to retrain my brain to think positive. I tried to keep my mind busy by reading a magazine. I only waited about ten minutes and the nurse called my name. I kept talking to myself telling myself I could do this.

Broken Inside…

Once inside the room I told Nurse Lori that I was having a little anxiety because the last time I was in there I had an anxiety attack. She told me I would be fine. I continued to tell her that I drove myself there today, something I haven't been able to do since December. She said she was proud of me. I got my blood pressure checked. It was a little high but the doctor assured me that he was not concerned by it. My anxiety made it a little higher than normal.

I began to tell the nurse and doctor how I've been doing since my last visit. The doctor agreed that the meds were working and that I was making progress. I told him of my fear of going back to work that I didn't feel I was ready yet. I told him that I didn't want him or anybody else to think I just didn't want to work. He said he never thought that and understood that I'm not ready to go back to work. I told him I feel like I'm on a time line and I have to be "cured" by a certain time. He said with this disorder there are no time limits to getting better. He wanted to see me in another month and would talk to the people at disability when they contact him.

I walked out of the office and into the car and said aloud, "I did it." "I did it." I was so proud of myself. I conquered this feat.

I then went to Kayli's doctor's office and picked up her physical form. When I went home I waited until it was time to take my mom to work then I took a three hour nap. I was completely, mentally drained from this. I needed to clear my mind so after my nap I felt refreshed.

Broken Inside…

It bothered me that my mom made the comment "you can't just sit home all day and watch television." That is the impression that she has. I feel like I'm trying my hardest to get through this disorder because at times I feel it tricks my brain into thinking the worst and I have to battle that within my head.

I explained that to her and now she understands. That's why keeping a journal is so important for me, so people don't think I'm just sitting around doing nothing.

April 22, 2007

I made it through this day. Today the kids had their last cheerleading competition of the season at Six Flags in Baltimore. It was a beautiful day and that made me feel good inside.

When we got there we parked up front close to the main gate so I could get to my truck quickly if I needed to. There weren't as many people there as I expected which I was happy about. It wasn't as big as I thought it would be either. I walked slowly and reminded myself I would be ok. I kept thinking positive thoughts.

The kids were able to get on a lot of rides since we didn't have to meet up with their teams until 4:00. The only ride I was able to get on was the rapids ride and of course Wayne had to go on with me. There weren't a lot of people waiting in line. Also, this wasn't a high thrill ride and I had been on one similar to this last year when I went to Dorney Park. I couldn't get on any other rides because I didn't want to have a panic attack on the roller coasters.

We went to the arena for their competition and I sat near the exit area. I was able to sit there for about an hour and a half then the girls got on a few more rides and we left about six thirty that evening. I was completely exhausted but I made it through the day without an anxiety attack.

I am learning to break everything I have to do into smaller increments and when I am able to get through the first little thing then I tell myself I can get through the next thing. I'm not obsessed with having to take my drink and snack everywhere like I used to but I never leave home without my Xanax. This is how I cope with my disorder.

April 24, 2007

Today I submitted my story to Readers Digest Magazine. I would love it if they would publish my story in their magazine. I have been going through a horrific experience and am triumphing over my situation as do so many of the other people whose stories are featured in their magazine. I pray that they choose my story.

April 25, 2007

I had a lot of anxiety while driving to therapy this morning. I was nervous and excited by seeing Karen this morning. I felt the waves of panic attacks coming on and dissipating. I kept telling myself I would be fine that I was just excited. Once I was there I still felt the anxiety. I told Karen what I was feeling. I took some deep breaths and proceeded to tell her how things were going since my last session.

April 30, 2007

I feel there may be success in my future after all. While watching the Montel Williams show this morning the show featured Kim Brecheen who is the president of a company called Slumber Parties, Inc. She talked about how she started the business. Similar to Tupperware and Mary Kay Parties, Slumber Parties sells sensual products to adults. I have been to one Slumber Party and have hosted two parties with another company so I was familiar with the parties.

She then talked about how she started a non-profit organization sponsored by Slumber Parties and its Distributors called SPARCAS (Slumber Parties Actively Restoring Character and Spirit). They posted the website so of course I went online to check it out. SPARCAS is geared toward women, especially mothers, who need support to keep their lives moving in the right direction. I downloaded the SPARCAS Assistance Application and realized that I meet the eligibility requirements which are: I am a female not associated with Slumber Parties, Inc., I currently hold a job (even though I've been on disability these few months), and I am a mother with my children living in the home. They strive to provide women with services that will build their families' characters, restore their spirits and empower their lives. I feel I can benefit from this. I filled out the form, attached a copy of my tax return, and included a letter explaining my situation.

I am a person who has struggled in so many ways throughout most of my life and hope to someday be able to share my story through my writing. I feel with a little help I may be able to accomplish a dream I've had since I was ten years old.

May 2, 2007

I contacted Readers Digest to find out how I would know if my story was chosen and published in their magazine. I was told that I would receive a letter in the mail. I visualize myself getting that letter in the mail and the feeling of accomplishing a goal if this happens.

Pray for me.

May 4, 2007

I made an appointment at Milford State Service Center for this afternoon. I went there to get assistance with paying my gas bill. I made sure the appointment would be at 3:00 so that Kristen could go with me. I was nervous about going by myself.

Broken Inside…

Once there Kristen waited out in the truck and I went inside by myself. I had my paperwork in order and I watched the TV while I waited. The intake worker called my name and I walked with her to her office. It wasn't far from the lobby. I sat down in her office and immediately noticed how adorable her office was. I was a little nervous when she shut the door but I could see outside the window and knew my truck wasn't far. I gave her all the information I brought with me and told her why we needed assistance with our gas bill.

At one point I mentioned that I was out on disability from my job. I proceeded to talk a little about my panic disorder and the agoraphobia. She said she thought she may have experienced some anxiety while going through her divorce. She also told me that she heard about people who couldn't leave their houses. I explained that my disorder was much more than that and at times I couldn't leave the house. She seemed empathetic. I asked her if she thought I was crazy. She didn't. I told her that I hadn't even talked to any of my coworkers about my situation. Other than family, my friend Martha was the only other person I had talked to about it.

During my intake process I asked her what her title was. She said she was a Social Services Technician. I asked her if the job required a degree and she stated, "No." Something inside me told myself that this would be a good job for me; that I could do this job. I made it through the appointment which lasted an hour.

Broken Inside…

When I went home I looked online for any Social Services Technician jobs. I didn't see any.

May 5, 2007

This morning my mom and I went to Lab Corp. to get our lab work done. I knew I wouldn't be able to go by myself. I was so afraid that I would have a panic attack in the middle of getting my blood drawn. While my mom and I were sitting in the waiting room one of the teachers from Charlton came in. I kept my head low so she wouldn't recognize me. I didn't want to have to face her.

When it came time for me to go back I was a little nervous. I have had my blood drawn many times but today I was afraid of the panic attack. As I sat in the chair waiting for the lady to draw my blood I kept telling myself I would be fine and it would only take a few minutes until I was done. I made it through without a panic attack. I was very happy.

I went into the next room with my mom and waited until she was done. I came home and felt like I walked a mile. I was mentally exhausted.

May 6, 2007

I went online to see if I could find any Social Services Technician positions available. I went on the State of Delaware website to check for the latest job openings. I found a FT Social

Services Technician position at a DHSS/Developmental Disabilities agency. I immediately updated my Resume and applied for the job online.

A part of me told myself that I would never get the job and the other part of me said if I were to get an interview I would go to the interview and see how it goes. From there I would determine if I would be able to take the position. I'm still not sure if I could get up Monday through Friday and work forty hours a week. I guess we'll see. They are taking applications until May 11th. I'm not getting my hopes up.

May 7, 2007

I had a lot of anxiety this morning. I was worried about what my lab results would be. Every year I have to have blood work done to check my TSH (Thyroid Stimulating Hormone) levels. I also wanted to have my cholesterol levels checked because I had heard if you have hypothyroidism you have an increased risk of high cholesterol.

I kept calling my doctor's office to get my results. Finally when I got a hold of the nurse she told me that my doctor wasn't in today so I would have to wait until tomorrow to get my test results. The knowing was one thing but the not knowing was worse.

I had myself convinced that my thyroid levels would be high indicating an increased dose of my Synthroid and that my cholesterol level was over 300. I had to go to the bank and almost turned around and drove straight home because of my anxiety. I convinced myself I would be ok. I told myself that I was worrying about my blood work and that was creating the anxiety. I told myself that I would be ok to go to the bank. For a split second I contemplated taking a Xanax but decided against it. I hadn't taken one in weeks. I went to the bank and was fine.

Later that afternoon I picked Kayli up from school and we went to Happy Harry's because I needed to use their copy machine. After I was finished I decided to check my blood pressure there. I shouldn't have because it was high for me. Knowing I didn't have the money I bought a blood pressure monitor because I had to know that I didn't have high blood pressure.

I went home and was happy to have the rest of the evening to relax. I had Kayli check my blood pressure twice and to my excitement it was normal. I was thrilled to know that I didn't suffer from high blood pressure. My anxiety was causing my blood pressure to be high.

May 8, 2007

This morning I felt the residual effects of anxiety. I wasn't sure what I was worried about. All day and night I had this feeling that I am on the cusp of something. In one sense I fear that I will be facing something that scares me and I will totally fall apart. In another sense I feel complete and total happiness is coming my way.

I'm so happy to report that my doctor's office phoned about the results of my blood work. My TSH levels were normal and my cholesterol levels were good.

After taking Kayli to school I was listening to this radio station. They had callers calling in to discuss their sexual abuse stories. Of course I was drawn into their stories.

One in particular was this man who was a police officer. He told of his being molested when he was five years old. While out on force one day he took a chair and busted it up side a man's head.

This man that he hit had apparently been molesting a little girl. The disc jockey asked the police officer if he ever went into therapy. He had stated that he tried once but didn't feel he was ready to deal with the abuse that happened to him.

The disc jockey told the man that although he wasn't a psychiatrist or therapist that he felt that he would benefit from therapy. He then told the man that "that little boy was who had taken the chair and busted it up against the assailant's head."

I found it interesting that he used this analogy because my therapist had used this same analogy in reference to my panic attacks. In a way because I had been ignoring my anxiety and hoping it would go away I wasn't acknowledging how I felt and in essence my panic attacks were like this scared little girl crying out for attention. When

Broken Inside…

Karen had first used it in this way I didn't understand the complexity of how true that is. I learned something about myself by listening to myself.

While lying in bed I really tried to tap into what was making me feel that I was on the "cusp" of something. After searching within myself I think that a part of me wants to get out in the work world and be a success and feel I deserve that and another part of me feels scared about that.

May 9, 2007

This morning I had a 9am appointment with Karen. My goal for today was to not experience any anxiety on the way to the appointment or during the appointment since my last visit I experienced a lot of anxiousness, nervousness, and anxiety while driving to my appointment. I got to my appointment a little early and began to read a magazine. I sat in the waiting room for about twenty minutes. During this time I assured myself that the last time I was there I was excited about all the new things I had to talk to her about. Today I felt calmer about being there.

Karen asked how I was doing. I told her that I felt I was making progress. I had been seriously contemplating going back to work but not just yet. I talked about me not being able to return to Charlton and the reasons why.

Broken Inside…

She asked what happened with my idea for selling the cheerleading gift baskets. I explained to her that first I needed to get a business license which requires money I didn't have and money to purchase the items that would go in the baskets to sell. Once I got my finances straight I would begin this venture.

Since my last visit I have been soul searching. I want desperately for success in the work field. I want to be one of those people who starts her own business and succeeds.

I told Karen about my idea to possibly work for Slumber Parties. Both of these jobs would only require a few hours of work or the weekends and I could work when I feel I am capable. I have been trying to visualize myself in different work environments and those two I think I could do. I at least have a plan.

I also informed her about SPARCAS. How I submitted my story to them and I hoped that they would help me. We talked about my finances and how they contributed to my breakdown. I have always been stressed about money. I cannot balance a checkbook and always pay my bills late. My credit score is low and because of that I feel like a failure. Karen gave me information on "Purses to Portfolios" a service that helps women in Delaware to retain financial control. They offer free seminars. I decided that I would take charge of my finances and face them. I decided to give this a try. I would feel so much more competent if my finances were in order.

Broken Inside…

I felt good about my visit today. When I went home I got online and registered for an online course on "Money Choices" that will be available on Friday May 25th. I am looking forward to doing this.

May 11, 2007

I wanted to be able to go to the grocery store this morning by myself. After dropping Kayli off at school I told myself that I could drive to the Sav-A-Lot and if I felt any anxiety I would turn around and drive myself home. The Sav-A-Lot is bigger than Witt Bros. Market yet smaller than Walmart. For me it was the next step. I was afraid of walking around the store by myself. I was terrified of having a panic attack and having to leave a cart of groceries in the middle of the aisle. I told myself that my goal was to walk into the store and even if I was only able to buy one or two items that would be good enough. I could then leave. Once inside the store I was calm. I walked through the store slowly and kept looking where the door was. I told myself that I could leave anytime I wanted. This made me feel better so I was able to complete my grocery shopping. I managed to buy a cart's worth of groceries today. I loaded them into the truck all by myself. When I went home I put away all the groceries and still had enough energy to do my housework. Life is getting better.

Tonight was Kristen and Kayli's awards banquet in

Middletown. Wayne went with us and it was very nice. I didn't have any anxiety the whole time we were there. Have I conquered it once and for all?

May 13, 2007

While lying in bed I tried to reach my inner child by talking to "her." I feel a large part of me is still that scared little girl. I envisioned a small, naked body curled up in the fetal position with her back to the world. She is buried deep within me and I for the first time in my life "saw her."

I talked to her as if I were talking to my own daughter. I told her that she doesn't need to be scared. I would take care of her. There is a part of me that feels I have been abused in some way and that she is the only one who can unlock the mystery. By reassuring her that I can handle whatever happened in my past I hope she lets the memories appear. I wonder if the Missy (my nickname) that everyone around me sees is really just a façade. Was a part of me created to appear confident, determined, and in control to keep the real me hidden?

May 14, 2007

Although I am on short-term disability and it was extended until July 10, 2007 I have been contemplating going back to work these past few days. I have been looking for jobs online to see what jobs are available that I think I could do once I feel I can go back to work. I know that I won't be returning to my old job. I want to be able to work part-time or work from home initially. I don't want to just jump into a full-time job and have the anxiety start all over again.

While picking Kayli up from school this afternoon I saw someone that I worked with at Charlton. I hoped he wouldn't see me. I was afraid if he did he would ask me why I've been out of work since December. I guess I could just tell him I'm out for personal reasons. I just don't want to talk about it to people yet.

I received an email that I did not meet the qualifications for the job I applied for on-line. I'm not mad. It wasn't meant to be.

Tonight I dreamt that I was standing next to this guy who was a football player. *He was late teens, early twenties. His mom is standing behind him. He grabs my breasts and wouldn't let go. I grab his hand and tell him, "Please don't do that." I tell his mom I don't like that.* I wake up.

May 15, 2007

Kayli had a dentist appointment this afternoon and my mom went with me. She sat in the truck while I took Kayli inside. I didn't have any anxiety while I waited for her to finish her appointment. We then went to the store and produce stand. I felt like a normal person today because I was able to do all this with no anxiety.

Broken Inside...

Later on I got on the computer. While online I found a job that would be perfect for me to do; telephone solicitor. I will be given a list of phone numbers to call to solicit donations. I can do this from home. I get paid per donation. It's a start. I am meeting with the woman, Dee tomorrow.

May 16, 2007

I have reservations about meeting Dee today and having my interview. I am scared to drive the half hour there by myself and back. I haven't been around too many people since my disorder. The thought of being alone with this woman and having a panic attack scares me. I don't want her to look at me like I'm crazy. I told myself that I will drive there but if I feel anxiety I will call her and tell her I can't meet with her.

Once I got there I felt fine. I ended up talking with her for about half an hour. This was a big step for me. If I am to go back to work someday I will have to be able to face people. I left there and felt that I had accomplished a major task.

Kayli asked me if I'd go to her class trip to Washington, D.C. this Friday. I explained to her that I can't do that. I do not think I am ready to be on a bus with a lot of other children and teachers for the two hour ride there and back. As a parent chaperone I wouldn't want something to happen if I were responsible for watching other people's kids. I wouldn't want to be walking around in a museum or something and have a panic attack and not be able to leave on my own terms. She understood why I can't go and I feel I made the best decision.

May 17, 2007

While lying in my bed I closed my eyes and tried to reach my "inner child." As I drew closer to her I saw her look up at me. I took her hands and held her close. I said to her, "Do not be afraid. I am here to protect you." I told her when she's ready she can share with me her memories and whatever happened wasn't her fault. I held her close in my embrace as I wiped the tears from her face.

May 18, 2007

My mood reflects the day. It's dark and gloomy outside. The kind of day that looks like at any moment a storm will come rolling through. I am afraid to go to therapy. After dropping Kayli off at school this morning I started to feel the twangs of anxiety. When I got home I envisioned myself having a panic attack in the therapist's office. Some part of me didn't want me to go to therapy. I was afraid that I would have to face my "inner child" and with that brings up all those feelings of fear and anxiety. I felt depressed all morning. I called and canceled my appointment. I told the secretary I wasn't feeling well. That was true. I felt guilty about not going to therapy so I took a nap. I had to quiet the thoughts that kept telling me I was going to have a panic attack. I was madder at myself for being afraid. Later that afternoon I was able to pick Kayli up from school. At least I did that.

May 21, 2007

I dreamt that *a cop I knew was very nice to me. He instructed me to go to his house. Once there I knew he was doing inappropriate things with little kids.*

May 22, 2007

I decided that I want to take my story of my Panic Disorder with Agoraphobia and have it published. I'm finding out there are many people out there like me who suffer from this. Most of them never talk about it to anyone. A lot of times the person's own family members have no idea what is wrong with them and have no idea how to help them.

It's important that I get my story out there. This way living as I have for the past few months won't be for nothing.

May 23, 2007

Last night I dreamt *that I was lying in my bed. Wayne was lying next to me. I began to scream and shake my head. I felt as if my head were exploding from fear. I was pointing to the window on the right and telling Wayne that "they" were coming to get me.*

Broken Inside…

Are my dreams trying to tell me something? My nightmares
start out with someone at the end of my bed. I realize it's a man.
Then he's in my bed, grabbing me. I am screaming from fear. Is the
message getting clearer? Will I ever remember what happened to me?
Will I ever know the truth? Is this where my fear stems from?

I believe that I was abused as a child and I am beginning to
experience that fear all over again. I remembered what my therapist
said at my last few sessions about my "inner child." Before that I
didn't realize that each of us has an inner child, also known as our
"true self."

I am beginning to understand how growing up watching my
father abuse my mother I repressed my feelings of anger, fear, and
love. I went on the internet to research any information on the "inner
child." I was shocked to see how many articles there are on it. There
is such a thing as "Inner Child Therapy." The articles talk about how
to visualize yourself as that child, talk to that part of yourself, ask
questions, and give him/her the love and nurturing you would any
other child. I have already begun doing this work.

Until I can begin to work a full-time job I contacted an Avon
Representative about selling Avon. Today I began working as an
Avon Representative. I need desperately to feel a part of something
good. This work will enable me to make a little extra money without
having to get up and go to work everyday and be around people all
the time. I can put the catalogs out with my name on it and when

people want to order something all they have to do is call me. I then place the order on-line and contact them when it comes in. I am capable of doing that and it's a step closer to going back to work. I am starting to feel like a real person again.

When I told Kayli this she said, "Mom you are a real person."

May 24, 2007

I dreaded going to my doctor's appointment this morning. I knew I wouldn't be able to have my mom go with me because she had an eye appointment in Dover this morning. I spent all morning thinking positively. I told myself I would be fine there; I would not have a panic attack today. I worried about getting there and having a panic attack.

Once there I was a little nervous and I was shaking while I was sitting in the waiting room. I started to feel my heart rate increase. My body starting going numb and I felt cold and clammy. For a split second I contemplated walking out of the doctor's office and going home. I told myself I wasn't going to leave. I needed to do this. I took a deep breath and started to read a magazine to get my mind off the anxiety.

I was happy that Nurse Lori called me back. I felt comfortable with her. I told her I was having some anxiety. She said I would be fine. I asked her if she still experiences anxiety even though she is on medication. She assured me that she still has those days; that made me feel better. I told her how I've been doing and she was happy to hear I was doing better than the last time I was in. I was much calmer by the time the doctor came in the room.

He reported that I don't need an increase in my Prozac because he stated that I have made good progress in this short amount of time. He said the next step is up to me. I have to be the one to decide what's next in my life. He told me that I have to figure out what it is I want to do with the rest of my life. I did tell him that I was working as a telephone solicitor from home and I just started selling Avon. I told him for me this was a step in the right direction.

We both agreed that I would not be returning to Charlton. It was best for me and the children. He stated that there are many jobs out there but some are not for me. I agreed. I left the appointment feeling very happy that I was able to get through it without having a panic attack.

May 26, 2007

I was not looking forward to today. Wayne's sister Michelle was in a very serious car accident a few days ago and her condition is critical. This would be the first time we got to see her in the hospital. Because Kristen had to work she was not able to go with us. Wayne, Kayli, and I went to see Michelle at Christiana Hospital in Newark.

I was fine until I got to the parking lot. We were parked so far away from the main entrance. When we got into the hospital my heart was racing from fear. It wasn't a long walk to the elevators and she was on the second floor. We did have to wait about fifteen minutes out in the hall until visiting hours started.

I stood near the elevator in case I had to make an escape. Wayne knew I was having anxiety about being there. He assured me that I would be ok. I was afraid with Wayne seeing his sister in critical condition and me having anxiety one of us might not be able to drive home. Thankfully the fifteen minutes went fast and we walked into her room. I told Wayne I may not be able to stay long.

Once inside Wayne, Kayli, and I talked to Michelle and she was awake for a few minutes. She started to doze off to sleep so we left the room to talk to her nurse. After about fifteen minutes we decided to leave because Michelle was still asleep. Kayli and I walked out to the car by ourselves so that Wayne could have time to visit with his sister alone.

The entire time I was in the hospital I kept feeling like there was this invisible string connecting me to my truck and because of the far distance I kept feeling the string stretch; fearing it might break.

May 29, 2007

I have this burning desire to share my story with others. This disorder is not something people typically talk about. I never realized this disorder affected so many people. I thought it was something that just affected my family. I just figured there was something wrong with us. I feel it's up to me to bring this disorder to people's attention.

I contacted a few book stores in my area to see if they would stock my book. Once it's published I have to take it to them to see if they will stock it.

In the meantime I contacted the Harrington Journal Newspaper (my local newspaper) to see if they would do an article on me and the book I'm having published. I was excited that they said they will do an article on me once my book is complete and ready for sale. I am hoping the exposure will help with my book's sales. I figure if people know me than they will be more willing to read about what I've gone through these past five months. It would be too hard for me to sit everyone down and explain my story over and over again.

May 30, 2007

After dropping Kayli off at school this morning I drove to my therapy appointment. I had some anxiety about going because I had to cancel my last appointment due to my anxiety.

I didn't wait long for my session to begin but I did feel the beginnings of a panic attack coming on. I told myself that I would be ok and that I wasn't going to discuss anything that I wasn't comfortable dealing with right now.

Broken Inside…

There were two questions that I needed Karen to answer. The first one was, "In order for me to get better do I have to dig down inside and dredge up whatever is repressed?" The second one was, "If I am moving on with my life does that mean that I am ignoring that part of myself that is scared?"

When my session started I told her the real reason why I missed my last session. I told her about the anxiety and feeling like I wasn't ready to bring up the feelings I have. I needed to know that she would understand how I felt and would still continue to be my therapist if I have a day like that again.

We talked about how I am always scared to show emotions. I always hide my feelings. I've learned to stuff them down. What I didn't realize was the feelings I repressed I did so to survive my childhood. I've spent my entire life not wanting to face those feelings.

Karen explained to me that I have different parts of myself. I am a scared little girl, a determined person, a survivor, and a criticizer.

In order for me to get better I don't have to dredge up what's repressed. She said it's not her job to pull me along. She is there to walk with me during this time in my life. "We're on this journey together", she said. I have to remember to acknowledge how I feel and why I am feeling that way. I have to remind myself it's ok to be scared. I just need to let my "inner child" know that I will not ignore her and I will protect her. My biggest problem is ignoring whatever problem comes my way and hoping it goes away. I don't like facing my problems. This is the part of me that is scared and maybe a part of me felt the problem (whatever it was) was too big for me to face so to protect myself I shut down.

The most interesting part of therapy today was learning how the world sees our "Thinking Adult." Underneath there is the "wounded child." We also have a fighter whether overt or covert, and a critical voice. The critical voice constantly verbally abuses the wounded child and makes her feel worse. In my case I've dealt with that part of myself for years. No matter what the situation, on one hand I can think I am determined, smart, pretty or whatever and my critical voice tells me that I should always be afraid, I am stupid, and I am ugly. I battle that in my head everyday.

Part of the reason why I haven't accomplished the goals I've had for myself is because I listen to that critical voice all the time. I am learning how to control that.

I read an article titled "Inner Child Discovery & Recovery – 5 Step Journey to Healing the Wounded Warrior" that I found very interesting. It states "the concept of inner children simply represents all of our emotions." *Think about that*. That makes sense to me. It goes on to say, "the inner adult, who is the equivalent to our higher power, represents those parts of ourselves that meets all responsibilities." That's true. Also, "the adult is responsible for becoming and being the perfect listener and validator for the inner children. The inner critic is detrimental to our inner children. It doesn't say anything kind or loving…..it criticizes and judges and continues to make us feel badly about ourselves. The adult will be responsible for the tools that are needed to STOP the inner critic. I definitely need help with this.

Level 1 – "Awareness", I need to remember to be aware of "what" I am feeling. The inner child (ren) represents my emotions. When I have thoughts in my head I need to know "who" is speaking; the critic, the child, or the adult. I need to be clear as to who is who. I am learning to be aware of my feelings now. When I have the thoughts in my head I know it's the critic and the inner child speaking. As the adult I tend to listen to them. I need to work on this.

Level 2 - "Relationship", Learning to use the "tools" that the adult is responsible for keeping the inner critic away and accessing and identifying the inner child(ren) easily and effectively. This will help to allow myself to develop a new and beautiful relationship with myself. I am working on this already some.

Level 3 - "Letting Go" states that once Levels 1 and 2 are securely in place, it is easy for the inner children to "let go" of those fears that I have been hanging on to, because the inner strength of the adult supports them. This is probably the hardest step for me. I had to learn to admit that I had fears and that it's ok to be afraid. Now I know I need to "let go" of them by reminding myself that I will be ok in whatever situation. I will talk myself through each situation I encounter.

Level 4 - "Spiritual Awareness", I'm not here yet. The article talks about the inner child being a direct connection to our higher power (inner adult) and if our inner child is wounded and crying inside we cannot experience joy, peacefulness, and spiritual connectedness to the fullest. As the inner child begins to heal, the natural transition is one of spiritual growth. I realized that my therapy is no longer about getting rid of the anxiety and getting back to my old life it's about understanding my feelings, how they attributed to the anxiety, and healing myself so that I can have a new outlook on life.

Level 5 - "Spiritual Being", on this level I can live my life fully aware of my inner child, without an inner critic, the adult is in charge and I have complete awareness of my spiritual connectedness to the source of all that is. My highs are not so high and my lows are not so low. I will be able to handle life's challenges and crisis's with less difficulty. Although I'm not at this level yet I have been able to conquer my anxiety a lot better than before.

Another article that I found very interesting was, "Inner Child Healing Techniques" by Robert Burney. It states that "when we are reacting out of our childhood emotional wounds, then what we are feeling may have very little to do with the situation we are in or with the people with whom we are dealing in the moment." I understand this now. It also says, "Anytime we have a strong emotional reaction to something or someone – when a button is pushed and there is a lot of energy attached a lot of intensity – that means there is old stuff involved." While reading the article I learned, "it is the inner child who feels panic or terror or rage or hopelessness, not the adult."

I always thought I was afraid but now I realize it's my inner child who is afraid. I don't need to know why the "child" feels panic, terror, rage, or whatever feeling – it is important however to honor that those feelings are valid. I need to own and honor my feelings without being a victim of them.

The most important thing I have to remember is to learn discernment. For me this is the hardest thing to do. Learning to ask for help from people who are trustworthy can be hard for me because I have trust issues with people. I am glad that I found a counselor who doesn't judge me or criticize me.

Karen gave me another assignment to work on. My assignment is to write down all my goals. This means I will have to do some soul searching because I don't know what I want out of my life. I guess the next step is for me to figure out what's next for me.

When I got home from therapy I saw on the caller id that someone from Charlton had called. I checked the messages. Denise had left me a message telling me that I needed to go into the school and have my evaluation done.

Broken Inside...

I called Denise back and I asked her why I had to have my evaluation done when I haven't been at work for almost five months. She stated that I was still an employee and Pam had to turn mine in. She wanted to know if I could come in today.

I told her I was very nervous about coming back to Charlton because I haven't talked to anybody there since before Christmas. I knew that I wasn't ready to go there today.

I told her that I wouldn't be able to come in today. She asked if I could possibly come in tomorrow. I said that it was a possibility. I then told her about me having the Panic Disorder and I may not be able to come in but I would try. She said she understood what I was going through and that I'd be surprised how many people at work cared about me. It felt so good to hear that. I had felt so much guilt being out of work all these months. I thought everybody was mad at me.

May 31, 2001

All morning I felt this strong desire to go to Charlton. I wanted so desperately for the understanding and support of my friends at work. I knew there were some people who genuinely cared about me and I needed to surround myself with them because I have isolated myself from them for so long.

There was this battle going on in my head and the child in me was winning. She wanted to be heard. She knew that my friends would want to know how I was doing. The adult side of me was afraid to face the people at work. I was afraid of what they thought of me. Somehow my "inner child" was embracing me and letting me know it would be ok.

After dropping Kayli off at school I felt that I was ready to go into work. I was hoping there would be people outside doing bus duty and that would make the transition of walking into the building a little easier. Unfortunately when I got there I had to walk in on my own.

As I walked through the door my emotions got the best of me. I saw Tammy and she hugged me. I told her I was so nervous about being there. She told me to be strong and hold my head up high. She said I didn't have anything to worry about.

I saw a few of my friends as I was heading to the main office. It felt so good to have people hug me and tell me they missed me. They asked if I was coming back to work and I replied, "No, I'm just here for a minute." That was my intention; get through the evaluation and leave.

When I walked into Pam's office I thought I was going to have a panic attack. I took a deep breath and told her I was so nervous. Talking to her I was shaking uncontrollably and almost in tears. I apologized for being a bad person and bad staff and for missing work for the past five months. I told her a little of what I was going through.

Broken Inside…

She explained that she knew people who were going through something similar to what I've been going through. She assured me that she understood.

I told her that I had no intention of coming back this summer. If I decided that I wouldn't be coming back for the next school year I needed to send her a letter so the school district could post my position. I will have to add that to my list of things to do.

I felt relieved when it was time to leave her office. Once I got that out of the way I went to thank Denise and talk to Ruth R. They seemed very empathetic when I shared with them about me having the Panic Disorder.

I decided to go say hello to Amy and Michelle. I wanted to make sure Amy wasn't mad at me for not being there all these months. She said she wasn't. I actually was able to sit down in my old classroom and visit with the kids. As I observed the children I knew I wasn't cut out for this type of work anymore and I was ok with that. I felt good about the visit.

On my way out of the building I saw one of the students I worked with last year. She had a big smile on her face. I gave her a hug and asked her teacher if I could go visit one of the other students in his class that I had worked with last year. He said, "Yes." I took the student's hand and we walked to her classroom. I said hello to the other student. I was so happy to see her. She remembered me but didn't quite remember my name. Mr. White told me they both have been doing well and I was proud of the progress they had made. I was glad I got to see them again.

I stopped in a few classes to say hello to some of my other friends. Everyone seemed very tickled to see me. One in particular, Janie, had some understanding of what was wrong with me. She stated that most people thought I was out of work for depression. I explained that what I had was a little more serious than that. We got to talking and I shared with her some of the things I had been going through. I felt comfortable talking to her. She said she admired me for being able to survive this ordeal and be a stronger person because of it.

I did reveal my intention of having this book published to a few of my friends. They promised me they will purchase it once it's available for sale.

I was invited to go to Franco's Restaurant with a few of my friends later that evening. I did meet up with them. It was so wonderful to be around people and not feel like I was being ostracized. I promised them I would keep in touch. I faced my fear of facing everyone at work and I conquered that fear.

While reading the Harrington Journal at home that night I read that the town of Felton will be having a Family Fun Day in September. The organizers are looking for authors for book signings. I think I would like to do that once my book's published. I will contact them about that.

June 1, 2007

Today started out ok. I was signed up to volunteer at the Dover Downs Racetrack to work the admissions gate this morning. Kayli's cheerleading squad asks each parent to participate in one fundraiser a year. I figured that I could handle this. I picked this day to work because there are less people there than on Saturday and Sunday's races.

When I thought about it I decided to have Kristen work it with me. I didn't want to be by myself. I convinced her to take the day off school and go with me. She drove there and the closer we got to Dover the more anxiety I felt. Three separate times I felt myself about to have a panic attack. The sheer magnitude of what was expected of me terrified me. I knew there would be a lot of people there. I knew I was expected to be there. I knew I couldn't just leave when I wanted to. I worried that I wouldn't be parked near the gate and I wouldn't be able to escape if I needed to.

I told Kristen what I was feeling and she told me I would be fine. I'm glad that she was with me because if she wasn't I would've turned the truck around and went home. I took many deep breaths and contemplated taking a Xanax but quickly decided not to.

I started to calm down once we turned into the Dover Downs parking lot. Luckily we found a parking spot near the gate we were working at. As I looked around I realized there weren't many people there at eight thirty in the morning. It was a short walk to the gate.

Broken Inside…

Once I saw some of the other Nitros parents I felt better. Because we weren't very busy I was able to occupy my mind by talking about Avon. Two of the parents placed orders with me. We then talked about the upcoming cheerleading season. Time went fast and before I knew it one o'clock came and it was time for us to leave.

This was my first attempt at "working" since before Christmas. I needed to see how I could handle volunteering at the races before actually committing myself to a job. From there I picked Kayli up from school early on my way to take Kristen to work. I went home and relaxed the rest of the afternoon.

Today I am writing down my future goals. After sharing my story I would love to be a motivational speaker on this disorder. Once my financial situation is better I will begin my cheerleader gift basket business. In the meantime I will continue selling Avon and working for Purple Heart. I will be proud of the success I've made and continue to make.

Although I am not cured I am getting my life back and that's progress. With Cognitive Therapy, Behavioral Therapy, Exposure Therapy, Inner Child Therapy, Medication, and following the Seven Keys to Overcoming Anxiety I will get better. Each day I follow "The Sedona Method" and "The Secret." I have the support of my family and some close friends and that is crucial for my success.

I'm not sure what the future holds for me; I take it a day at a time. If I relapse I will not beat myself up about it. I will take the time to look at my life and my actions to see what may have caused me to have anxiety. I am learning to listen to my body whereas before I ignored what was going on inside me.

I am at a turning point in my life right now. As much as I want to better myself and my situation by being a better person to the outside world I realized that I have a lot more work to do on the "inside." I am up for the challenge. This will be the next step in my therapy; healing my inner child and releasing the inner critic so that the adult can be in charge. I will nurture myself from now on.

This book was written to bring to light the devastation that this anxiety disorder had and still has on me. There are many others who suffer from anxiety disorders and are not heard. Each person's story is different. If you know of anyone who is suffering from any type of anxiety disorder don't assume their crazy or that it's just all in their mind. This is a real disorder. Show them love, support, and understanding. Many people do not seek treatment.

Broken Inside...

Encourage anyone you know with an anxiety disorder to seek help. I'm glad I did.

Broken Inside…

www.ingramcontent.com/pod-product-compliance
Lightning Source LLC
Chambersburg PA
CBHW020301290526
45784CB00003B/1320